Learning Human

Learning Human

selected poems

Les Murray

farrar . straus . giroux | new york

Farrar, Straus and Giroux
19 Union Square West, New York 10003

Copyright © 1998 by Les Murray
All rights reserved
Distributed in Canada by Douglas & McIntyre Ltd.
Printed in the United States of America
Designed by Debbie Glasserman
First published in 1998 by Duffy & Snellgrove, Australia
First published in the United States by Farrar, Straus and Giroux
First edition, 2000

Library of Congress Cataloging-in-Publication Data
Murray, Les A., 1938–
    Learning human : selected poems / Les Murray. — 1st ed.
      p.   cm.
    Includes index.
    ISBN 0-374-26073-7 (alk. paper)
    I. Title.
PR9619.3.M83A6   2000
821—dc21   99-42758

Contents

Learning Human

The Burning Truck

for Mrs. Margaret Welton

It began at dawn with fighter planes:
they came in off the sea and didn't rise,
they leaped the sandbar one and one and one
coming so fast the crockery they shook down
off my kitchen shelves was spinning in the air
when they were gone.

They came in off the sea and drew a wave
of lagging cannon-shells across our roofs.
Windows spat glass, a truck took sudden fire,
out leaped the driver, but the truck ran on,
growing enormous, shambling by our street-doors,
coming and coming . . .

By every right in town, by every average
we knew of in the world, it had to stop,
fetch up against a building, fall to rubble
from pure force of burning, for its whole
body and substance were consumed with heat
but it would not stop.

And all of us who knew our place and prayers
clutched our verandah-rails and window-sills,
begging that truck between our teeth to halt,
keep going, vanish, strike . . . but set us free.
And then we saw the wild boys of the street
go running after it.

And as they followed, cheering, on it crept,
windshield melting now, canopy-frame a cage
torn by gorillas of flame, and it kept on
over the tramlines, past the church, on past
the last lit windows, and then out of the world
with its disciples.

Driving Through Sawmill Towns

1

In the high cool country,
having come from the clouds,
down a tilting road
into a distant valley,
you drive without haste. Your windscreen parts the forest,
swaying and glancing, and jammed midday brilliance
crouches in clearings . . .
then you come across them,
the sawmill towns, bare hamlets built of boards
with perhaps a store,
perhaps a bridge beyond
and a little sidelong creek alive with pebbles.

2

The mills are roofed with iron, have no walls:
you look straight in as you pass, see lithe men working,

the swerve of a winch,
dim dazzling blades advancing
through a trolley-borne trunk
till it sags apart
in a manifold sprawl of weatherboards and battens.

The men watch you pass:
when you stop your car and ask them for directions,
tall youths look away—
it is the older men who
come out in blue singlets and talk softly to you.

Beside each mill, smoke trickles out of mounds
of ash and sawdust.

3

You glide on through town,
your mudguards damp with cloud.
The houses there wear verandahs out of shyness,
all day in calendared kitchens, women listen
for cars on the road,
lost children in the bush,
a cry from the mill, a footstep—
nothing happens.

The half-heard radio sings
its song of sidewalks.

Sometimes a woman, sweeping her front step,
or a plain young wife at a tankstand fetching water
in a metal bucket will turn round and gaze
at the mountains in wonderment,
looking for a city.

4

Evenings are very quiet. All around
the forest is there.
As night comes down, the houses watch each other:
a light going out in a window here has meaning.

You speed away through the upland,
glare through towns
and are gone in the forest, glowing on far hills.

On summer nights
ground-crickets sing and pause.
In the dark of winter, tin roofs sough with rain,
downpipes chafe in the wind, agog with water.
Men sit after tea
by the stove while their wives talk, rolling a dead match
between their fingers,
thinking of the future.

An Absolutely Ordinary Rainbow

The word goes round Repins,
the murmur goes round Lorenzinis,
at Tattersalls, men look up from sheets of numbers,
the Stock Exchange scribblers forget the chalk in their hands
and men with bread in their pockets leave the Greek Club:
There's a fellow crying in Martin Place. They can't stop him.

The traffic in George Street is banked up for half a mile
and drained of motion. The crowds are edgy with talk
and more crowds come hurrying. Many run in the back streets
which minutes ago were busy main streets, pointing:
There's a fellow weeping down there. No one can stop him.

The man we surround, the man no one approaches
simply weeps, and does not cover it, weeps
not like a child, not like the wind, like a man
and does not declaim it, nor beat his breast, nor even
sob very loudly—yet the dignity of his weeping

holds us back from his space, the hollow he makes about him
in the midday light, in his pentagram of sorrow,
and uniforms back in the crowd who tried to seize him
stare out at him, and feel, with amazement, their minds
longing for tears as children for a rainbow.

Some will say, in the years to come, a halo
or force stood around him. There is no such thing.
Some will say they were shocked and would have stopped him
but they will not have been there. The fiercest manhood,
the toughest reserve, the slickest wit amongst us

trembles with silence, and burns with unexpected
judgements of peace. Some in the concourse scream
who thought themselves happy. Only the smallest children
and such as look out of Paradise come near him
and sit at his feet, with dogs and dusty pigeons.

Ridiculous, says a man near me, and stops
his mouth with his hands, as if it uttered vomit—
and I see a woman, shining, stretch her hand
and shake as she receives the gift of weeping;
as many as follow her also receive it

and many weep for sheer acceptance, and more
refuse to weep for fear of all acceptance,
but the weeping man, like the earth, requires nothing,
the man who weeps ignores us, and cries out
of his writhen face and ordinary body

not words, but grief, not messages, but sorrow,
hard as the earth, sheer, present as the sea—
and when he stops, he simply walks between us
mopping his face with the dignity of one
man who has wept, and now has finished weeping.

Evading believers, he hurries off down Pitt Street.

Vindaloo in Merthyr Tydfil

The first night of my second voyage to Wales,
tired as rag from ascending the left cheek of Earth,
I nevertheless went to Merthyr in good company
and warm in neckclothing and speech in the Butcher's Arms
till Time struck us pintless, and Eddie Rees steamed in brick lanes
and under the dark of the White Tip we repaired shouting

to I think the Bengal. I called for curry, the hottest,
vain of my nation, proud of my hard mouth from childhood,
the kindly brown waiter wringing the hands of dissuasion
O vindaloo, sir! You sure you want vindaloo, sir?
But I cried Yes please, being too far in to go back,
the bright bells of Rhymney moreover sang in my brains.

Fair play, it was frightful. I spooned the chicken of Hell
in a sauce of rich yellow brimstone. The valley boys with me
tasting it, croaked to white Jesus. And only pride drove me,
forkful by forkful, observed by hot mangosteen eyes,
by all the carnivorous castes and gurus from Cardiff
my brilliant tears washing the unbelief of the Welsh.

Oh it was a ride on Watneys plunging red barrel
through all the burning ghats of most carnal ambition
and never again will I want such illumination
for three days on end concerning my own mortal coil
but I signed my plate in the end with a licked knife and fork
and green-and-gold spotted, I sang for my pains like the free
before I passed out among all the stars of Cilfynydd.

Incorrigible Grace

Saint Vincent de Paul, old friend,
my sometime tailor,
I daresay by now you are feeding
the rich in Heaven.

Boöpis

(from "Walking to the Cattle Place")

Coming out of reflections
I find myself in the earth.
My cow going on
into the creek from this paspalum-thatched tunnel-track
divides her hoofs among the water's impediments,
clastic and ungulate stones.
She is just deep
enough to be suckling the stream when she drinks from it.

Wetted hooves, like hers,
incised in the alluvium
this grave's-width ramp up through the shoulder of the bank
but cattle paunches with their tongue-mapped girths also
brushed in glazes,
easements and ample places
at the far side of things from subtractive plating of spades
or the vertical slivers a coffin will score, sinking.

North, the heaped districts, and south
there'd be at least a Pharaoh's destruction of water
suspended above me in this chthonic section.
Seeds fall in here from the poise
of ploughland, grass land.
I could be easily
foreclosed to a motionless size in the ruins of gloss.

The old dead, though, are absorbed, becoming strata.
The crystals, too, of glaze or matt, who have
not much say in a slump
seem coolly balanced toward me.
At this depth among roots
I thank God's own sacrifice
that I am not here with seeds and a weighty request
from the upper fields,
my own words constrained with a cord.

Not being that way, if I met the lady of summer,
the beautiful cow-eyed one, I would be saying:

Madam, the children of the overworld
cannot lay down their instruments at will.
Babel in orbit maps the hasty parks,
missile and daisy scorn the steady husbands
and my countrymen mix green with foreign fruit.

The Pure Food Act

(from "Walking to the Cattle Place")

Night, as I go into the place of cattle.

Night over the dairy
the strainers sleeping in their fractions,
vats
and the mixing plunger, that dwarf ski-stock, hung.

On the creekstone cement
water driven hard through the Pure Food Act
dries slowest round tree-segment stools,
each buffed
to a still bum-shine,
sides calcified with froth.

Country disc-jocks
have the idea. Their listeners aren't all human.
Cows like, or let their milk for, a firm beat
nothing too plangent (diesel bass is good).
Sinatra, though, could calm a yardful of horns
and the Water Music
has never yet corrupted honest milkers
in their pure food act.

The quiet dismissal switching it off, though,
and carrying the last bucket, saline-sickly
still undrinkable raw milk to pour in high
for its herringbone and cooling pipe-grid
fall
to the muscle-building cans.

His wedding, or a war,
might excuse a man from milking
but milk-steeped hands are good for a violin
and a cow in rain time is
a stout wall of tears.

But I'm britching back.

I let myself out through the bail gate.
Night, as I say.
Night, as I go out to the place of cattle.

■ József

M.J.K. 1883–1974 In Piam Memoriam

You ride on the world-horse once
no matter how brave your seat
or polished your boots, it may gallop you
into undreamed-of fields

but this field's outlandish: Australia!
To end in this burnt-smelling, blue-hearted
metropolis of sore feet and trains
(though the laughing bird's a good fellow).

Outlandish not to have died
in king-and-kaiserly service,
dismounted, beneath the smashed guns
or later, with barons and credit

after cognac, a clean pistol death.
Alas, a small target, this heart.
Both holes were in front, though, entry
and exit. I learned to relish that.

Strange not to have died with the Kingdom
when Horthy's fleet sank, and the betting
grew feverish, on black and on red,
to have outlived even my Friday club

and our joke: *senilis senili
gaudet.* I bring home coffee now.
Dear God, not one café in this place,
no Andrássy-street, no Margaret's Island . . .

no law worth the name: they are British
and hangmen and precedent-quibblers
make rough jurisprudence at best.
Fairness, of course; that was their word.

I don't think Nature speaks English.
I used to believe I knew enough
with *gentleman, whisky, handicap*
and perhaps *tweed*. French lacked all those.

I learned the fine detail at seventy
out here. Ghosts in many casinos
must have smiled as I hawked playing cards
to shady clubs up long stairways

and was naturalized by a Lord Mayor
and many bookmakers, becoming a
New Australian. My son claims he always
was one. We had baptized him Gino

in Hungary. His children are natives
remote as next century. My eyes
are losing all faces, all letters,
the colours go, red, white, now green

into Hungary, Hungary of the poplar trees
and the wide summers where I am young
in uniform, riding with Nelly,
the horseshoes' noise cupping our speeches.

I, Mórelli József Károly,
once attorney, twice gunshot, thrice rich,
my cigarettes, monogrammed, from Kyriazi,
once married (dear girl!) to a Jew

(gaining little from that but good memories
though my son's uniforms fitted her son
until it was next year in Cape Town),
am no longer easy to soften.

I will eat stuffed peppers and birds' milk,
avoid nuns, who are monstrous bad luck,
write letters from memory, smoke Winstons
and flex my right elbow at death

and, more gently, at living.

Kiss of the Whip

In Cardiff, off Saint Mary's Street,
there in the porn shops you could get
a magazine called Kiss of the Whip.
I used to pretend I'd had poems in it.

Kiss of the Whip. I never saw it.
I might have encountered familiar skills
having been raised in a stockwhip culture.
Grandfather could dock a black snake's head,

Stanley would crack the snake for preference
leap from his horse grab whirl and jolt!
the popped head hummed from his one-shot slingshot.
The whips themselves were black, fine-braided,

arm-coiling beasts that could suddenly flourish
and cut a cannibal strip from a bull
(millisecond returns) or idly behead an
ant on the track. My father did that.

A knot in the lash would kill a rabbit.
There were decencies: good dogs and children
were flogged with the same lash doubled back.
A horsehair plait on the tip for a cracker

sharpened the note. For ten or twelve thousand
years this was the sonic barrier's
one human fracture. Whip-cracking is that:
thonged lightning making the leanest thunder.

When black snakes go to Hell they are
affixed by their fangs to carved whip-handles
and fed on nothing but noonday heat,
sweat and flowing rumps and language.

They writhe up dust-storms for revenge
and send them roaring where creature comfort's

got with a touch of the lash. And that
is a temple yard that will bear more cleansing

before, through droughts and barracks, those
lax, quiet-speaking, sudden fellows
emerge where skill unbraids from death
and mastering, in Saint Mary's Street.

The Broad Bean Sermon

Beanstalks, in any breeze, are a slack church parade
without belief, saying *trespass against us* in unison,
recruits in mint Air Force dacron, with unbuttoned leaves.

Upright with water like men, square in stem-section
they grow to great lengths, drink rain, keel over all ways,
kink down and grow up afresh, with proffered new greenstuff.

Above the cat-and-mouse floor of a thin bean forest
snails hang rapt in their food, ants hurry through several dimensions:
spiders tense and sag like little black flags in their cordage.

Going out to pick beans with the sun high as fence-tops, you find
plenty, and fetch them. An hour or a cloud later
you find shirtfulls more. At every hour of daylight

appear more than you missed: ripe, knobbly ones, fleshy-sided,
thin-straight, thin-crescent, frown-shaped, bird-shouldered,
    boat-keeled ones,
beans knuckled and single-bulged, minute green dolphins at suck,

beans upright like lecturing, outstretched like blessing fingers
in the incident light, and more still, oblique to your notice
that the noon glare or cloud-light or afternoon slants will uncover

till you ask yourself Could I have overlooked so many, or
do they form in an hour? unfolding into reality
like templates for subtly broad grins, like unique caught expressions,

like edible meanings, each sealed around with a string
and affixed to its moment, an unceasing colloquial assembly,
the portly, the stiff, and those lolling in pointed green slippers . . .

Wondering who'll take the spare bagfulls, you grin with happiness
—it is your health—you vow to pick them all
even the last few, weeks off yet, misshapen as toes.

The Mitchells

I am seeing this: two men are sitting on a pole
they have dug a hole for and will, after dinner, raise
I think for wires. Water boils in a prune tin.
Bees hum their shift in unthinning mists of white

bursaria blossom, under the noon of wattles.
The men eat big meat sandwiches out of a styrofoam
box with a handle. One is overheard saying:
drought that year. Yes. Like trying to farm the road.

The first man, if asked, would say *I'm one of the Mitchells.*
The other would gaze for a while, dried leaves in his palm,
and looking up, with pain and subtle amusement,

say *I'm one of the Mitchells.* Of the pair, one has been rich
but never stopped wearing his oil-stained felt hat. Nearly
   everything
they say is ritual. Sometimes the scene is an avenue.

▊ The Powerline Incarnation

When I ran to snatch the wires off our roof
hands bloomed teeth shouted I was almost seized
held back from this life
                              O flumes   O chariot reins
you cover me with lurids deck me with gaudies feed
my coronal   a scream sings in the air
above our dance   you slam it to me with farms
that you dark on and off numb hideous strong friend
Tooma and Geehi freak and burr through me
rocks fire-trails damwalls mountain-ash trees slew
to darkness through me   I zap them underfoot
with the swords of my shoes
                                    I am receiving mountains
piloting around me   Crackenback   Anembo
the Fiery Walls   I make a hit in towns
I've never visited: smoke curls lightbulbs pop grey
discs hitch and slow   I plough the face of Mozart
and Johnny Cash   I bury and smooth their song
I crack it for copper links and fusebox spiders
I call my Friend from the circuitry of mixers
whipping cream for a birthday   I distract the immortal
Inhuman from hospitals
                              to sustain my jazz
and here is Rigel in a glove of flesh
my starry hand discloses smoke, cold Angel.

Vehicles that run on death come howling into
our street with lights a thousandth of my blue
arms keep my wife from my beauty   from my species
the jewels in my tips
                              I would accept her in
blind white remarriage   cover her with wealth
to arrest the heart   we'd share Apache leaps
crying out *Disyzygy!*
                              shield her from me, humans
from this happiness I burn to share   this touch
sheet car   live ladder   wildfire garden shrub—

away off I hear the bombshell breakers thrown
diminishing me   a meaninglessness coming
over the circuits
                    the god's deserting me
but I have dived in the mainstream   jumped the graphs
I have transited the dreams of crew-cut boys named Buzz
and the hardening music
                        to the big bare place
where the strapped-down seekers, staining white clothes, come
to be shown the Zeitgeist
                        passion and death my skin
my heart all logic   I am starring there
and must soon flame out
                        having seen the present god
It who feels nothing   It who answers prayers.

Creeper Habit

On Bennelong Point
a two-dimensional tree
drapes the rock cutting.

Bird-flecked, self-espaliered
it issues out of the kerb
feeding on dead sparks
of the old tram depot;

a fig, its muscles
of stiffened chewing gum grip
the flutings and beads
of the crowbar-and-dynamite wall.

The tree has height and extent
but no roundness. Cramponned in cracks
its branches twine and utter
coated leaves.

With half its sky blank rock
it has little choice.
It has climbed high from a tiny sour gall

and spreads where it can,
feeding its leaves on the light
of North Shore windows.

Employment for the Castes in Abeyance

I was a translator at the Institute:
fair pay, clean work, and a bowerbird's delight
of theory and fact to keep the forebrain supple.

I was Western Europe. *Beiträge, reviste,
dissertaties, rapports* turned English under my
one-fingered touch. Teacup-and-Remington days.

It was a job like Australia: peace and cover,
a recourse for exiles, poets, decent spies,
for plotters who meant to rise from the dead with their circle.

I was getting over a patch of free-form living:
flat food round the midriff, long food up your sleeves—
castes in abeyance, we exchanged these stories.

My Chekhovian colleague who worked as if under surveillance
would tell me tales of real life in Peking and Shanghai
and swear at the genders subsumed in an equation.

The trade was uneasy about computers, back then:
if they could be taught not to render, say, *out of sight
out of mind* as *invisible lunatic*

they might supersede us—not
because they'd be better. More on principle.
Not that our researchers were unkindly folk:

one man on exchange from Akademgorod
told me about Earth's crustal plates, their ponderous
inevitable motion, collisions that raised mountain chains,

the continents rode on these Marxian turtles, it seemed;
another had brought slow death to a billion rabbits,
a third team had bottled the essence of rain on dry ground.

They were translators, too, our scientists:
they were translating the universe into science,
believing that otherwise it had no meaning.

Leaving there, I kept my Larousse and my Leutseligkeit
and I heard that machine translation never happened:
language defeated it. We are a language species.

I gather this provoked a shift in science,
that having become a side, it then changed sides
and having collapsed, continued at full tempo.

Prince Obolensky succeeded me for a time
but he soon returned to Fiji to teach Hebrew.
In the midst of life, we are in employment:

seek, travel and print, seek-left-right-travel-and-bang
as the Chinese typewriter went which I saw working
when I was a translator in the Institute.

The Buladelah-Taree Holiday Song Cycle

1

The people are eating dinner in that country north of
    Legge's Lake;
behind flywire and venetians, in the dimmed cool, town people
    eat Lunch.
Plying knives and forks with a peek-in sound, with a tuck-in
    sound,
they are thinking about relatives and inventory, they are talking
    about customers and visitors.
In the country of memorial iron, on the creek-facing hills there,
they are thinking about bean plants, and rings of tank water, of
    growing a pumpkin by Christmas;
rolling a cigarette, they say thoughtfully Yes, and their companion
    nods, considering.
Fresh sheets have been spread and tucked tight, childhood rooms
    have been seen to,
for this is the season when children return with their children
to the place of Bingham's Ghost, of the Old Timber Wharf, of the
    Big Flood That Time,
the country of the rationalized farms, of the day-and-night farms,
    and of the Pitt Street farms,
of the Shire Engineer and many other rumours, of the tractor
    crankcase furred with chaff,
the places of sitting down near ferns, the snake-fear places, the
    cattle-crossing-long-ago places.

2

It is the season of the Long Narrow City; it has crossed the Myall,
    it has entered the North Coast,
that big stunning snake; it is looped through the hills, burning all
    night there.
Hitching and flying on the downgrades, processionally balancing
    on the climbs,
it echoes in O'Sullivan's Gap, in the tight coats of the flooded-
    gum trees;
the tops of palms exclaim at it unmoved, there near Wootton.

Glowing all night behind the hills, with a north-shifting glare,
    burning behind the hills;
through Coolongolook, through Wang Wauk, across the Wallamba,
the booming tarred pipe of the holiday slows and spurts again;
    Nabiac chokes in glassy wind,
the forests on Kiwarrak dwindle in cheap light; Tuncurry and
    Forster swell like cooking oil.
The waiting is buffed, in timber villages off the highway, the
    waiting is buffeted:
the fumes of fun hanging above ferns; crime flashes in strange
    windscreens, in the time of the Holiday.
Parasites weave quickly through the long gut that paddocks shine
    into;
powerful makes surging and pouncing: the police, collecting
    Revenue.
The heavy gut winds over the Manning, filling northward,
    digesting the towns, feeding the towns;
they all become the narrow city, they join it;
girls walking close to murder discard, with excitement, their
    names.
Crossing Australia of the sports, the narrow city, bringing home
    the children.

3

It is good to come out after driving and walk on bare grass;
walking out, looking all around, relearning that country.
Looking out for snakes, and looking out for rabbits as well;
going into the shade of myrtles to try their cupped climate,
    swinging by one hand around them,
in that country of the Holiday . . .
stepping behind trees to the dam, as if you had a gun,
to that place of the Wood Duck,
to that place of the Wood Duck's Nest,
proving you can still do it; looking at the duck who hasn't seen you,
the mother duck who'd run Catch Me (broken wing) I'm Fatter
    (broken wing), having hissed to her children.

4

The birds saw us wandering along.
Rosellas swept up crying out *we think we think*; they settled farther
    along;
knapping seeds off the grass, under dead trees where their eggs
    were, walking around on their fingers,
flying on into the grass.
The heron lifted up his head and elbows; the magpie stepped aside
    a bit,
angling his chopsticks into pasture, turning things over in his head.
At the place of the Plough Handles, of the Apple Trees Bending
    Over, and of the Cattlecamp,
there the vealers are feeding; they are loosely at work, facing
    everywhere.
They are always out there, and the forest is always on the hills;
around the sun are turning the wedgetail eagle and her mate, that
    dour brushhook-faced family:
they settled on Deer's Hill away back when the sky was opened,
in the bull-oak trees way up there, the place of fur tufted in the
    grass, the place of bone-turds.

5

The Fathers and the Great-grandfathers, they are out in the
    paddocks all the time, they live out there,
at the place of the Rail Fence, of the Furrows Under Grass, at the
    place of the Slab Chimney.
We tell them that clearing is complete, an outdated attitude, all
    over;
we preach without a sacrifice, and are ignored; flowering bushes
    grow dull to our eyes.
We begin to go up on the ridge, talking together, looking at the
    kino-coloured ants,
at the yard-wide sore of their nest, that kibbled peak, and the
    workers heaving vast stalks up there,
the brisk compact workers; jointed soldiers pour out then, tense
    with acid; several probe the mouth of a lost gin bottle;
Innuendo, we exclaim, *literal minds!* and go on up the ridge,
    announced by finches;
passing the place of the Dingo Trap, and that farm hand it caught,
    and the place of the Cowbails,

we come to the road and watch heifers,
little unjoined Devons, their teats hidden in fur, and the cousin
     with his loose-slung stockwhip driving them.
We talk with him about rivers and the lakes; his polished horse is
     stepping nervously,
printing neat omegas in the gravel, flexing its skin to shake off
     flies;
his big sidestepping horse that has kept its stones; it recedes
     gradually, bearing him;
we murmur *stone-horse* and *devilry* to the grinners under grass.

6

Barbecue smoke is rising at Legge's Camp; it is steaming into the
     midday air,
all around the lake shore, at the Broadwater, it is going up among
     the paperbark trees,
a heat-shimmer of sauces, rising from tripods and flat steel, at that
     place of the cone shells,
at that place of the Seagrass, and the tiny segmented things
     swarming in it, and of the Pelican.
Dogs are running around disjointedly; water escapes from their
     mouths,
confused emotions from their eyes; humans snarl at them
     Gwanout and Hereboy, not varying their tone much;
the impoverished dog people, suddenly sitting down to nuzzle
     themselves; toddlers side with them:
toddlers, running away purposefully at random, among cars, into
     big drownie water (come back, Cheryl-Ann!).
They rise up as charioteers, leaning back on the tow-bar; all their
     attributes bulge at once:
swapping swash shoulder-wings for the white-sheeted shoes that
     bear them,
they are skidding over the flat glitter, stiff with grace, for once not
     travelling to arrive.
From the high dunes over there, the rough blue distance, at length
     they come back behind the boats,
and behind the boats' noise, cartwheeling, or sitting down, into the
     lake's warm chair;
they wade ashore and eat with the families, putting off that
     uprightness, that assertion,

eating with the families who love equipment, and the freedom
    from equipment,
with the fathers who love driving, and lighting a fire between
    stones.

7

Shapes of children were moving in the standing corn, in the child-
    labour districts;
coloured flashes of children, between the green and parching
    stalks, appearing and disappearing.
Some places, they are working, racking off each cob like a lever,
    tossing it on the heaps;
other places, they are children of child-age, there playing jungle:
in the tiger-striped shade, they are firing hoehandle machine-guns,
    taking cover behind fat pumpkins;
in other cases, it is Sunday and they are lovers.
They rise and walk together in the sibilance, finding single rows
    irksome, hating speech now,
or, full of speech, they swap files and follow defiles, disappearing
    and appearing;
near the rain-grey barns, and the children building cattleyards
    beside them;
the standing corn, gnawed by pouched and rodent mice;
    generations are moving among it,
the parrot-hacked, medicine-tasseled corn, ascending all the creek
    flats, the wire-fenced alluvials,
going up in patches through the hills, towards the Steep Country.

8

Forests and State Forests, all down off the steeper country;
    mosquitoes are always living in there:
they float about like dust motes and sink down, at the places of
    the Stinging Tree,
and of the Staghorn Fern; the males feed on plant-stem fluid,
    absorbing that watery ichor;
the females meter the air, feeling for the warm-blooded smell,
    needing blood for their eggs.
They find the dingo in his sleeping-place, they find his underbelly
    and his anus;

they find the possum's face, they drift up the ponderous pleats of
    the fig tree, way up into its rigging,
the high camp of the fruit bats; they feed on the membranes and
    ears of bats; tired wings cuff air at them;
their eggs burning inside them, they alight on the muzzles of
    cattle,
the half-wild bush cattle, there at the place of the Sleeper Dump,
    at the place of the Tallowwoods.
The males move about among growth tips; ingesting solutions,
    they crouch intently;
the females sing, needing blood to breed their young; their singing
    is in the scrub country;
their tune comes to the name-bearing humans, who dance to it
    and irritably grin at it.

9

The warriors are cutting timber with brash chainsaws; they are
    trimming hardwood pit-props and loading them;
Is that an order? they hoot at the peremptory lorry driver, who
    laughs; he is also a warrior.
They are driving long-nosed tractors, slashing pasture in the
    dinnertime sun;
they are fitting tappers and valves, the warriors, or giving finish to
    a surfboard.
Addressed on the beach by a pale man, they watch waves break
    and are reserved, refusing pleasantry;
they joke only with fellow warriors, chaffing about try-ons and
    the police, not slighting women.
Making Timber a word of power, Con-rod a word of power, Sense
    a word of power, the Regs. a word of power,
they know belt-fed from spring-fed; they speak of being *stiff*, and
    being *history*;
the warriors who have killed, and the warriors who eschewed
    killing,
the solemn, the drily spoken, the life peerage of endurance;
    drinking water from a tap,
they watch boys who think hard work a test, and boys who think
    it is not a test.

10

Now the ibis are flying in, hovering down on the wetlands,
on those swampy paddocks around Darawank, curving down in
    ragged dozens,
on the riverside flats along the Wang Wauk, on the Boolambayte
    pasture flats,
and away towards the sea, on the sand moors, at the place of the
    Jabiru Crane;
leaning out of their wings, they step down; they take out their
    implement at once,
out of its straw wrapping, and start work; they dab grasshopper
    and ground-cricket
with nonexistence . . . spiking the ground and puncturing it . . .
    they swallow down the outcry of a frog;
they discover titbits kept for them under cowmanure lids, small
    slow things.
Pronging the earth, they make little socket noises, their
    thoughtfulness jolting down and up suddenly;
there at Bunyah, along Firefly Creek, and up through Germany,
the ibis are all at work again, thin-necked ageing men towards
    evening; they are solemnly all back
at Minimbah, and on the Manning, in the rye-and-clover
    irrigation fields;
city storemen and accounts clerks point them out to their wives,
remembering things about themselves, and about the ibis.

11

Abandoned fruit trees, moss-tufted, spotted with dim lichen paints;
    the fruit trees of the Grandmothers,
they stand along the creekbanks, in the old home paddocks, where
    the houses were,
they are reached through bramble-grown front gates, they creak at
    dawn behind burnt skillions,
at Belbora, at Bucca Wauka, away in at Burrell Creek,
at Telararee of the gold-sluices.
The trees are split and rotten-elbowed; they bear the old-fashioned
    summer fruits,
the annual bygones: china pear, quince, persimmon;
the fruit has the taste of former lives, of sawdust and parlour song,
    the tang of Manners;

children bite it, recklessly,
at what will become for them the place of the Slab Wall, and of
    the Coal Oil Lamp,
the place of moss-grit and swallows' nests, the place of the
    Crockery.

12

Now the sun is an applegreen blindness through the swells, a
    white blast on the sea face, flaking and shoaling;
now it is burning off the mist; it is emptying the density of trees, it
    is spreading upriver,
hovering above the casuarina needles, there at Old Bar and
    Manning Point;
flooding the island farms, it abolishes the milkers' munching
    breath
as they walk towards the cowyards; it stings a bucket here, a
    teatcup there.
Morning steps into the world by ever more southerly gates;
    shadows weaken their north skew
on Middle Brother, on Cape Hawke, on the dune scrub toward
    Seal Rocks;
steadily the heat is coming on, the butter-water time, the clothes-
    sticking time;
grass covers itself with straw; abandoned things are thronged with
    spirits;
everywhere wood is still with strain; birds hiding down the creek
    galleries, and in the cockspur canes;
the cicada is hanging up her sheets; she takes wing off her music-
    sheets.
Cars pass with a rational zoom, panning quickly towards
    Wingham,
through the thronged and glittering, the shale-topped ridges, and
    the cattlecamps,
towards Wingham for the cricket, the ball knocked hard in front
    of smoked-glass ranges, and for the drinking.
In the time of heat, the time of flies around the mouth, the time
    of the west verandah;
looking at that umbrage along the ranges, on the New England
    side;

clouds begin assembling vaguely, a hot soiled heaviness on the sky,
    away there towards Gloucester;
a swelling up of clouds, growing there above Mount George, and
    above Tipperary;
far away and hot with light; sometimes a storm takes root there,
    and fills the heavens rapidly;
darkening, boiling up and swaying on its stalks, pulling this way
    and that, blowing round by Krambach;
coming white on Bulby, it drenches down on the paddocks, and
    on the wire fences;
the paddocks are full of ghosts, and people in cornbag hoods
    approaching;
lights are lit in the house; the storm veers mightily on its stem,
    above the roof; the hills uphold it;
the stony hills guide its dissolution; gullies opening and crumbling
    down, wrenching tussocks and rolling them;
the storm carries a greenish-grey bag; perhaps it will find hail and
    send it down, starring cars, flattening tomatoes,
in the time of the Washaways, of the dead trunks braiding water,
    and of the Hailstone Yarns.

13

The stars of the holiday step out all over the sky.
People look up at them, out of their caravan doors and their
    campsites;
people look up from the farms, before going back; they gaze at
    their year's worth of stars.
The Cross hangs head-downward, out there over Markwell;
it turns upon the Still Place, the pivot of the Seasons, with one
    shoulder rising:
"Now I'm beginning to rise, with my Pointers and my Load . . ."
hanging eastwards, it shines on the sawmills and the lakes, on the
    glasses of the Old People.
Looking at the Cross, the galaxy is over our left shoulder, slung up
    highest in the east;
there the Dog is following the Hunter; the Dog Star pulsing there
    above Forster; it shines down on the Bikies,
and on the boat-hire sheds, there at the place of the Oyster; the
    place of the Shark's Eggs and her Hide;

the Pleiades are pinned up high on the darkness, away back above
the Manning;
they are shining on the Two Blackbutt Trees, on the rotted river
wharves, and on the towns;
standing there, above the water and the lucerne flats, at the place
of the Families;
their light sprinkles down on Taree of the Lebanese shops, it
mingles with the streetlights and their glare.
People recover the starlight, hitching north,
travelling north beyond the seasons, into that country of the
Communes, and of the Banana:
the Flying Horse, the Rescued Girl, and the Bull, burning steadily
above that country.
Now the New Moon is low down in the west, that remote
direction of the Cattlemen,
and of the Saleyards, the place of steep clouds, and of the Rodeo;
the New Moon who has poured out her rain, the moon of the
Planting-times.
People go outside and look at the stars, and at the melon-rind
moon,
the Scorpion going down into the mountains, over there towards
Waukivory, sinking into the tree-line,
in the time of the Rockmelons, and of the Holiday . . .
the Cross is rising on his elbow, above the glow of the horizon;
carrying a small star in his pocket, he reclines there brilliantly,
above the Alum Mountain, and the lakes threaded on the Myall
River, and above the Holiday.

The Gum Forest

(from "Four Gaelic Poems")

After the last gapped wire on a post,
homecoming for me, to enter the gum forest.

This old slow battlefield: parings of armour,
cracked collars, elbows, scattered on the ground.

New trees step out of old: lemon and ochre
splitting out of grey everywhere, in the gum forest.

In there for miles, shade track and ironbark slope,
depth casually beginning all around, at a little distance.

Sky sifting, and always a hint of smoke in the light;
you can never reach the heart of the gum forest.

In here is like a great yacht harbour, charmed to leaves,
innumerable tackle, poles wrapped in spattered sail,
or an unknown army in reserve for centuries.

Flooded-gums on creek ground, each tall because of each.
Now a blackbutt in bloom is showering with bees
but warm blood sleeps in the middle of the day.
The witching hour is noon in the gum forest.

Foliage builds like a layering splash: ground water
drily upheld in edge-on, wax-rolled, gall-puckered
leaves upon leaves. The shoal life of parrots up there.

Stone footings, trunk-shattered. Non-human lights. Enormous
abandoned machines. The mysteries of the gum forest.

Delight to me, though, at the water-smuggling creeks,
health to me, too, under banksia candles and combs.

A wind is up, rubbing limbs above the bullock roads;
mountains are waves in the ocean of the gum forest.

I go my way, looking back sometimes, looking round me;
singed oils clear my mind, and the pouring sound high up.

Why have I denied the passions of my time? To see
lightning strike upward out of the gum forest.

Rainwater Tank

Empty rings when tapped give tongue,
rings that are tense with water talk:
as he sounds them, ring by rung,
Joe Mitchell's reddened knuckles walk.

The cattledog's head sinks down a notch
and another notch, beside the tank,
and Mitchell's boy, with an old jack-plane,
lifts moustaches from a plank.

From the puddle that the tank has dripped
hens peck glimmerings and uptilt
their heads to shape the quickness down;
petunias live on what gets spilt.

The tankstand spider adds a spittle
thread to her portrait of her soul.
Pencil-grey and stacked like shillings
out of a banker's paper roll

stands the tank, roof-water drinker.
The downpipe stares drought into it.
Briefly the kitchen tap turns on
then off. But the tank says Debit, Debit.

The Future

There is nothing about it. Much science fiction is set there
but is not about it. Prophecy is not about it.
It sways no yarrow stalks. And crystal is a mirror.
Even the man we nailed on a tree for a lookout
said little about it; he told us evil would come.
We see, by convention, a small living distance into it
but even that's a projection. And all our projections
fail to curve where it curves.
                                   It is the black hole
out of which no radiation escapes to us.
The commonplace and magnificent roads of our lives
go on some way through cityscape and landscape
or steeply sloping, or scree, into that sheer fall
where everything will be that we have ever sent there,
compacted, spinning—except perhaps us, to see it.
It is said we see the start.
                                   But, from here, there's a blindness.
The side-heaped chasm that will swallow all our present
blinds us to the normal sun that may be imagined
shining calmly away on the far side of it, for others
in their ordinary day. A day to which all our portraits,
ideals, revolutions, denim and deshabille
are quaintly heartrending. To see those people is impossible,
to greet them, mawkish. Nonetheless, I begin:
"When I was alive—"
                                   and I am turned around
to find myself looking at a cheerful picnic party,
the women decently legless, in muslin and gloves,
the men in beards and weskits, with the long
cheroots and duck trousers of the better sort,
relaxing on a stone verandah. Ceylon, or Sydney.
And as I look, I know they are utterly gone,
each one on his day, with pillow, small bottles, mist,
with all the futures they dreamed or dealt in, going
down to that engulfment everything approaches;
with the man on the tree, they have vanished into the Future.

Immigrant Voyage

My wife came out on the *Goya*
in the mid-year of our century.

In the fogs of that winter
many hundred ships were sounding;
the DP camps were being washed to sea.

The bombsites and the ghettoes
were edging out to Israel,
to Brazil, to Africa, America.

The separating ships were bound away
to the cities of refuge
built for the age of progress.

Hull-down and pouring light
the tithe-barns, the cathedrals
were bearing the old castes away.

Pattern-bombed out of babyhood,
Hungarians-become-Swiss,
the children heard their parents:
Argentina? Or Australia?
Less politics, in Australia . . .

Dark Germany, iron frost
and the waiting many weeks
then a small converted warship
under the moon, turning south.

Way beyond the first star
and beyond Cape Finisterre
the fishes and the birds
did eat of their heave-offerings.

The *Goya* was a barracks:
mess-queue, spotlights, tower,
crossing the Middle Sea.

In the haunted blue light
that burned nightlong in the sleeping-decks
the tiered bunks were restless
with coughing, demons, territory.

On the Sea of Sweat, the Red Sea,
the flat heat melted even
dulled deference of the injured.
Nordics and Slavonics
paid salt-tax day and night, being
absolved of Europe

but by the Gate of Tears
the barrack was a village
with accordions and dancing
(Fräulein, kennen Sie meinen Rhythmus?)
approaching the southern stars.

Those who said Europe
has fallen to the Proles
and the many who said
we are going for the children,

the nouveau poor
and the cheerful shirtsleeve Proles,
the children, who thought
No Smoking signs meant men
mustn't dress for dinner,

those who had hopes
and those who knew that they
were giving up their lives

were becoming the people
who would say, and sometimes urge,

in the English-speaking years:
We came out on the *Goya*.

At last, a low coastline,
old horror of Dutch sail-captains.

Behind it, still unknown,
sunburnt farms, strange trees, family jokes
and all the classes of equality.

As it fell away northwards
there was one last week for songs,
for dreaming at the rail,
for beloved meaningless words.

Standing in to Port Phillip
in the salt-grey summer light
the village dissolved
into strained shapes holding luggage;

now they, like the dour
Australians below them, were facing
encounter with the Foreign
where all subtlety fails.

Those who, with effort,
with concealment, with silence, had resisted
the collapsed star Death,
who had clawed their families from it,
those crippled by that gravity

were suddenly, shockingly
being loaded aboard lorries:
They say, another camp—
One did not come for this—

As all the refitted
ships stood, oiling, in the Bay,

spectres, furious and feeble,
accompanied the trucks through Melbourne,

resignation, understandings
that cheerful speed dispelled at length.

That first day, rolling north
across the bright savanna,
not yet people, but numbers.
Population. Forebears.

Bonegilla, Nelson Bay,
the dry land barbed-wire ships
from which some would never land.

In these, as their parents
learned the Fresh Start music:
physicians nailing crates,
attorneys cleaning trams,
the children had one last
ambiguous summer holiday.

Ahead of them lay
the Deep End of the schoolyard,
tribal testing, tribal soft-drinks,
and learning English fast,
the Wang-Wang language.

Ahead of them, refinements:
thumbs hooked down hard under belts
to repress gesticulation;

ahead of them, epithets:
wog, reffo, Commo Nazi,
things which can be forgotten
but must first be told.

And farther ahead
in the years of the Coffee Revolution

and the Smallgoods Renaissance,
the early funerals:

the misemployed, the unadaptable,
those marked by the Abyss,

friends who came on the *Goya*
in the mid-year of our century.

Homage to the Launching-place

Pleasure-craft of the sprung rhythms, bed,
            kindest of quadrupeds,
you are also the unrocking boat
            that moves on silence.

Straining hatchway into this world,
            you sustain our collapses
above earth; guarantor of evolution,
            you are our raised base-line.

Resisting gravity, for us and in us,
            you form a planet-wide
unobtrusive discontinuous platform,
            a layer: the mattressphere,
pretty nearly our highest common level
            (tables may dispute it).

            Muscles' sweatprinted solace,
godmother of butt-stubbing dreams,
            you sublimate, Great Vehicle,
all our upright passions;
            midwife of figuring, and design,
you moderate them wisely;
            aiming solitude outwards, at action,
you sigh Think some more. Sleep on it . . .

Solitude. Approaching rest
Time reveals her oscillation
            and narrows into space;
            there is time in that dilation:
            Mansions. Defiles. Continents.
            The living and the greatly living,
            objects that take sides,
            that aren't morally neutral—

you accept my warm absence
            there, as you will accept,
one day, my cooling presence.

I loved you from the first, bed,
doorway out of this world;
        above your inner springs
I learned to dig my own.

        Primly dressed, linen-collared one,
you look so still, for your speed,
            shield that carries us to the fight
            and bears us from it.

First Essay on Interest

Not usury, but interest. The cup slowed in mid-raise,
the short whistle, hum, the little forwards shift
mark our intake of that non-physical breath

which the lungs mimic sharply, to cancel the gap in pressure
left by our self vanishing into its own alert—
A blink returns us to self, that intimate demeanour

self-repairing as a bow-wave. What we have received
is the ordinary mail of the otherworld, wholly common,
not postmarked divine; no one refuses delivery,

not even the eagle, her face fixed at heavy Menace:
I have juices to sort the relevant from the irrelevant;
even her gaze may tilt left, askance, aloof, right,
fixing a still unknown. Delaying huge flight.

Interest. Mild and inherent with fire as oxygen,
it is a sporadic inhalation. We can live long days
under its surface, breathing material air

then something catches, is itself. Intent and special silence.
This is interest, that blinks our interests out
and alone permits their survival, by relieving

us of their gravity, for a timeless moment;
that centres where it points, and points to centring,
that centres us where it points, and reflects our centre.

It is a form of love. The everyday shines through it
and patches of time. But it does not mingle with these;
it wakens only for each trace in them of the Beloved.

And this breath of interest is non-rhythmical:
it is human to obey, humane to be wary of rhythm
as tainted by the rallies, as marching with the snare drum.
The season of interest is not fixed in the calendar cycle;

it pulls towards acute dimensions. Death is its intimate.
When that Holland of cycles, the body, veers steeply downhill
interest retreats from the face; it ceases to instill
and fade, like breath; it becomes a vivid steady state

that registers every grass-blade seen on the way,
the long combed grain in the steps, free insects flying;
it stands aside from your panic, the wracked disarray;
it behaves as if it were the part of you not dying.

Affinity of interest with extremity
seems to distil to this polar disaffinity
that suggests the beloved is not death, but rather
what our death has hidden. Which may be this world.

The Fishermen at South Head

They have walked out as far as they can go on the prow of the
    continent,
on the undercut white sandstone, the bowsprits of the towering
    headland.
They project their long light canes
or raise them up to check and string, like quiet archers.
Between casts they hold them couched,
a finger on the line, two fingers on a cigarette, the reel cocked.

They watch the junction of smooth blue with far matt-shining
    blue,
the join where clouds enter,
or they watch the wind-shape of their nylon
bend like a sail's outline
south towards, a mile away, the city's floating gruel
of gull-blown effluent.

Sometimes they glance north, at the people on that calf-coloured
    edge
lower than theirs, where the suicides come by taxi
and stretchers are winched up
later, under raining lights
but mostly their eyes stay level with the land-and-ocean glitter.

Where they stand, atop the centuries
of strata, they don't look down much
but feel through their tackle the talus-eddying
and tidal detail of that huge simple pulse
in the rock and in their bones.

It feels good. It feels right.
The joy of sitting high is in our judgement.
The marvellous brute-force effects of our century work.
They answer something in us. Anything in us.

View of Sydney, Australia, from Gladesville Road Bridge
(from "The Sydney Highrise Variations")

There's that other great arch eastward, with its hanging highways;
the headlands and horizons of packed suburb, white among
     bisque-fired; odd smokes rising;
there's Warrang, the flooded valley, that is now the ship-chained
     Harbour,
recurrent everywhere, with its azure and its grains;
ramped parks, bricked containers,
verandahs successive around walls,
and there's the central highrise, multi-storey, the twenty-year
     countdown,
the new city standing on its haze above the city.

> Ingots of sheer
> affluence poles
> bomb-drawing grid
> of columnar profit
> piecrust and scintillant
> tunnels in the sky
> high window printouts
> repeat their lines
> repeat their lines
> credit conductors
> repeat their lines
> bar graphs on blue
> glass tubes of boom
> in concrete wicker
> each trade Polaris
> government Agena
> fine print insurrected
> tall things on a tray

All around them is the old order: brewery brick terrace hospital
horrible workplace; the scale of the tramway era,
the peajacket era, the age of the cliff-repeating woolstores.
South and west lie the treeless suburbs, a mulch of faded flags,
north and partly east, the built-in paradise forest.

Quintets for Robert Morley

Is it possible that hyper–
ventilating up Parnassus
I have neglected to pay tribute
to the Stone Age aristocracy?
    I refer to the fat.

We were probably the earliest
civilized, and civilizing, humans,
the first to win the leisure,
sweet boredom, life-enhancing sprawl
    that require style.

Tribesfolk spared us and cared for us
for good reasons. Our reasons.
As age's counterfeits, forerunners of the city,
we survived, and multiplied. Out of self-defence
    we invented the Self.

It's likely we also invented some of love,
much of fertility (see the Willensdorf Venus)
parts of theology (divine feasting, Unmoved Movers)
likewise complexity, stateliness, the ox-cart
    and self-deprecation.

Not that the lists of pugnacity are bare
of stout fellows. Ask a Sumo.
Warriors taunt us still, and fear us:
in heroic war, we are apt to be the specialists
    and the generals.

But we do better in peacetime. For ourselves
we would spare the earth. We were the first moderns
after all, being like the Common Man
disqualified from tragedy. Accessible to shame, though,
    subtler than the tall,

we make reasonable rulers.
Never trust a lean meritocracy
nor the leader who has been lean;
only the lifelong big have the knack of wedding
    greatness with balance.

Never wholly trust the fat man
who lurks in the lean achiever
and in the defeated, yearning to get out.
He has not been through our initiations,
    he lacks the light feet.

Our having life abundantly
is equivocal, Robert, in hot climates
where the hungry watch us. I lack the light step then too.
How many of us, I wonder, walk those streets
    in terrible disguise?

So much climbing, on a spherical world;
had Newton not been a mere beginner at gravity
he might have asked how the apple got up there
in the first place. And so might have discerned
    an ampler physics.

▌ Equanimity

Nests of golden porridge shattered in the silky-oak trees,
cobs and crusts of it, their glory-box;
the jacarandas' open violet immensities
mirrored flat on the lawns,
weighted by sprinklers; birds, singly and in flocks
hopping over the suburb, eating, as birds do, in detail
and paying their peppercorns;
talk of "the good life" tangles love with will
however; if we mention it, there is more to say:
the droughty light, for example, at telephone-wire
height above the carports, not the middle-ground
distilling news-photograph light of a smoggy Wednesday,
but that light of the north-west wind, hung on the sky
like the haze above cattleyards;
hungry mountain birds, too, drifting in for food, with the sound
of moist gullies about them, and the sound of the pinch-bar;
we must hear the profoundly unwished
garble of a neighbours' quarrel, and see repeatedly
the face we saw near the sportswear shop today
in which mouth-watering and tears couldn't be distinguished.

Fire-prone place-names apart
there is only love; there are no Arcadias.
Whatever its variants of meat-cuisine, worship, divorce,
human order has at heart
an equanimity. Quite different from inertia, it's a place
where the churchman's not defensive, the indignant aren't on the
       qui vive,
the loser has lost interest, the accountant is truant to remorse,
where the farmer has done enough struggling-to-survive
for one day, and the artist rests from theory—
where all are, in short, off the high comparative horse
of their identity.
Almost beneath notice, as attainable as gravity, it is
a continuous recovering moment. Pity the high madness
that misses it continually, ranging without rest between
assertion and unconsciousness,

the sort that makes Hell seem a height of evolution.
Through the peace beneath effort
(even within effort: quiet air between the bars of our attention)
comes unpurchased lifelong plenishment;
Christ spoke to people most often on this level
especially when they chattered about kingship and the Romans;
all holiness speaks from it.

From the otherworld of action and media, this
interleaved continuing plane is hard to focus:
we are looking into the light—
it makes some smile, some grimace.
More natural to look at the birds about the street, their life
that is greedy, pinched, courageous and prudential
as any on these bricked tree-mingled miles of settlement,
to watch the unceasing on-off
grace that attends their nearly every movement,
the same grace moveless in the shapes of trees
and complex in our selves and fellow walkers: we see it's indivisible
and scarcely willed. That it lights us from the incommensurable
that we sometimes glimpse, from being trapped in the point
(bird minds and ours are so pointedly visual):
a field all foreground, and equally all background,
like a painting of equality. Of infinite detailed extent
like God's attention. Where nothing is diminished by perspective.

Shower

From the metal poppy
this good blast of trance
arriving as shock, private cloudburst blazing down,
worst in a boarding-house greased tub, or a barrack with
    competitions,
best in a stall, this enveloping passion of Australians:
tropics that sweat for you, torrent that braces with its heat,
inflames you with its chill, action sauna, inverse bidet,
sleek vertical coruscating ghost of your inner river,
reminding all your fluids, streaming off your points, awakening
the tacky soap to blossom and ripe autumn, releasing the squeezed
    gardens,
smoky valet smoothing your impalpable overnight pyjamas off,
pillar you can step through, force-field absolving love's efforts,
nicest yard of the jogging track, speeding aeroplane minutely
steered with two controls, or trimmed with a knurled wheel.
Some people like to still this energy and lie in it,
stirring circles with their pleasure in it—but my delight's that toga
worn on either or both shoulders, fluted drapery, silk whispering
    to the tiles
with its spiralling frothy hem continuous round the gurgle-hole;
this ecstatic partner, dreamy to dance in slow embrace with
after factory-floor rock, or even to meet as Lot's abstracted
merciful wife on a rusty ship in dog latitudes,
sweetest dressing of the day in the dusty bush, this persistent
time-capsule of unwinding, this nimble straight well-wisher.
Only in England is its name an unkind word;
only in Europe is it enjoyed by telephone.

The Quality of Sprawl

Sprawl is the quality
of the man who cut down his Rolls-Royce
into a farm utility truck, and sprawl
is what the company lacked when it made repeated efforts
to buy the vehicle back and repair its image.

Sprawl is doing your farming by aeroplane, roughly,
or driving a hitchhiker that extra hundred miles home.
It is the rococo of being your own still centre.
It is never lighting cigars with ten-dollar notes:
that's idiot ostentation and murder of starving people.
Nor can it be bought with the ash of million-dollar deeds.

Sprawl lengthens the legs; it trains greyhounds on liver and beer.
Sprawl almost never says Why not? with palms comically raised
nor can it be dressed for, not even in running shoes worn
with mink and a nose ring. That is Society. That's Style.
Sprawl is more like the thirteenth banana in a dozen
or anyway the fourteenth.

Sprawl is Hank Stamper in *Never Give an Inch*
bisecting an obstructive official's desk with a chainsaw.
Not harming the official. Sprawl is never brutal
though it's often intransigent. Sprawl is never Simon de Montfort
at a town-storming: Kill them all! God will know his own.
Knowing the man's name this was said to might be sprawl.

Sprawl occurs in art. The fifteenth to twenty-first
lines in a sonnet, for example. And in certain paintings;
I have sprawl enough to have forgotten which paintings.
Turner's glorious *Burning of the Houses of Parliament*
comes to mind, a doubling bannered triumph of sprawl—
except, he didn't fire them.

Sprawl gets up the nose of many kinds of people
(every kind that comes in kinds) whose futures don't include it.
Some decry it as criminal presumption, silken-robed Pope
    Alexander

dividing the new world between Spain and Portugal.
If he smiled *in petto* afterwards, perhaps the thing did have sprawl.

Sprawl is really classless, though. It's John Christopher Frederick
    Murray
asleep in his neighbours' best bed in spurs and oilskins
but not having thrown up:
sprawl is never Calum who, drunk, along the hallways of our
    house,
reinvented the Festoon. Rather
it's Beatrice Miles going twelve hundred ditto in a taxi,
No Lewd Advances, No Hitting Animals, No Speeding,
on the proceeds of her two-bob-a-sonnet Shakespeare readings.
An image of my country. And would that it were more so.

No, sprawl is full-gloss murals on a council-house wall.
Sprawl leans on things. It is loose-limbed in its mind.
Reprimanded and dismissed
it listens with a grin and one boot up on the rail
of possibility. It may have to leave the Earth.
Being roughly Christian, it scratches the other cheek
and thinks it unlikely. Though people have been shot for sprawl.

Weights

Not owning a cart, my father
in the drought years was a bowing
green hut of cattle feed, moving,
or gasping under cream cans. No weight
would he let my mother carry.

Instead, she wielded handles
in the kitchen and dairy, singing often,
gave saucepan-boiled injections
with her ward-sister skill, nursed neighbours,
scorned gossips, ran committees.

She gave me her factual tone,
her facial bones, her will,
not her beautiful voice
but her straightness and her clarity.

I did not know back then
nor for many years what it was,
after me, she could not carry.

Midsummer Ice

Remember how I used
to carry ice in from the road
for the ice chest, half running,
the white rectangle clamped in bare hands
the only utter cold
in all those summer paddocks?

How, swaying, I'd hurry it inside
en bloc and watering, with the butter
and the wrapped bread precarious on top of it?
"Poor Leslie," you would say,
"your hands are cold as charity—"
You made me take the barrow
but uphill it was heavy.

We'd no tongs, and a bag
would have soaked and bumped, off balance.
I loved to eat the ice,
chip it out with the butcher knife's grey steel.
It stopped good things rotting
and it had a strange comb at its heart,
a splintered horizon rife with zero pearls.

But you don't remember.
A doorstep of numbed creek water the colour of tears
but you don't remember.
I will have to die before you remember.

Machine Portraits with Pendant Spaceman

For Valerie

The bulldozer stands short as a boot on its heel-high ripple soles;
it has toecapped stumps aside all day, scuffed earth and trampled
    rocks
making a hobnailed dyke downstream of raw clay shoals.
Its work will hold water. The man who bounced high on the box
seat, exercising levers, would swear a full frontal orthodox
oath to that. First he shaved off the grizzled scrub
with that front-end safety razor supplied by the school of hard
    knocks
then he knuckled down and ground his irons properly; they
    copped many a harsh rub.
At knock-off time, spilling thunder, he surfaced like a sub.

Speaking of razors, the workshop amazes with its strop,
its elapsing leather drive-belt angled to the slapstick flow
of fast work in the Chaplin age; tightened, it runs like syrup,
streams like a mill-sluice, fiddles like a glazed virtuoso.
With the straitlaced summary cut of Sam Brownes long ago
it is the last of the drawn lash and bullocking muscle
left in engineering. It's where the panther leaping, his swift
    shadow
and all such free images turned plastic. Here they dwindle, dense
    with oil,
like a skein between tough factory hands, pulley and diesel.

Shaking in slow low flight, with its span of many jets,
the combine seeder at nightfall swimming over flat land
is a style of machinery we'd imagined for the fictional planets:
in the high glassed cabin, above vapour-pencilling floodlights, a
    hand,
gloved against the cold, hunts along the medium-wave band
for company of Earth voices; it crosses speech garble music—
the Brandenburg Conch the Who the Illyrian High Command—
as seed wheat in the hoppers shakes down, being laced into the
    thick
night-dampening plains soil, and the stars waver out and stick.

Flags and a taut fence discipline the mountain pasture
where giant upturned mushrooms gape mildly at the sky
catching otherworld pollen. Poppy-smooth or waffle-ironed, each
    armature
distils wild and white sound. These, Earth's first antennae
tranquilly angled outwards, to a black, not a gold infinity,
swallow the millionfold numbers that print out as a risen
glorious Apollo. They speak control to satellites in high
bursts of algorithm. And some of them are tuned to win
answers to fair questions, viz. What is the Universe in?

How many metal-bra and trumpet-flaring film extravaganzas
underlie the progress of the space shuttle's Ground Transporter
    Vehicle
across macadam-surfaced Florida? Atop oncreeping house-high
    panzers,
towering drydock and ocean-liner decks, there perches a gridiron
    football
field in gradual motion; it is the god-platform; it sustains the bridal
skyscraper of liquid Cool, and the rockets borrowed from the
    Superman
and the bricked aeroplane of Bustout-and-return, all vertical,
conjoined and myth-huge, approaching the starred gantry where
    human
lightning will crack, extend, and vanish upwards from this caravan.

      Gold-masked, the foetal warrior
      unslipping on a flawless floor,
      I backpack air; my life machine
      breathes me head-Earthwards, speaks the Choctaw
      of tech-talk that earths our discipline—

      but the home world now seems outside-in;
      I marvel that here background's so fore
      and sheathe my arms in the unseen

      a dream in images unrecalled
      from any past takes me   I soar
      at the heart of fall on a drifting line

this is the nearest I have been
to oneness with the everted world
the unsinking leap   the stone unfurled

In a derelict village picture show I will find a projector,
dust-matted, but with film in its drum magazines, and the lens
mysteriously clean. The film will be called *Insensate Violence*,
no plot, no characters, just shoot burn scream beg claw
bayonet trample brains—I will hit the reverse switch then, in
     conscience,
and the thing will run backwards, unlike its coeval the machine-
     gun;
blood will unspill, fighters lift and surge apart; horror will be
     undone
and I will come out to a large town, bright parrots round the
     saleyard pens
and my people's faces healed of a bitter sophistication.

The more I act, the stiller I become;
the less I'm lit, the more spellbound my crowd;
I accept all colours, and with a warming hum
I turn them white and hide them in a cloud.
To give long life is a power I'm allowed
by my servant, Death. I am what you can't sell
at the world's end—and if you're still beetle-browed
try some of my treasures: an adult bird in its shell
or a pink porker in his own gut, Fritz the Abstract Animal.

No riddles about a crane. This one drops a black clanger on cars
and the palm of its four-thumbed steel hand is a raptor of
     wrecked tubing;
the ones up the highway hoist porridgy concrete, long spars
and the local skyline; whether raising aloft on a string
bizarre workaday angels, or letting down a rotating
man on a sphere, these machines are inclined to maintain
a peace like world war, in which we turn over everything
to provide unceasing victories. Now the fluent lines stop, and
     strain
engrosses this tower on the frontier of junk, this crane.

Before a landscape sprouts those giant stepladders that pump oil
or before far out iron mosquitoes attach to the sea
there is this sortilege with phones that plug into mapped soil,
the odd gelignite bump to shake trucks, paper scribbling out
    serially
as men dial Barrier Reefs long enfolded beneath the geology
or listen for black Freudian beaches; they seek a miles-wide
    pustular
rock dome of pure Crude, a St Paul's-in-profundis. There are
    many
wrong numbers on the geophone, but it's brought us some
    distance, and by car.
Every machine has been love and a true answer.

Not a high studded ship boiling cauliflower under her keel
nor a ghost in bootlaced canvas—just a length of country road
afloat between two shores, winding wet wire rope reel-to-reel,
dismissing romance sternwards. Six cars and a hay truck are her
    load
plus a thoughtful human cast which could, in some dramatic
    episode,
become a world. All machines in the end join God's creation
growing bygone, given, changeless—but a river ferry has its
    timeless mode
from the grinding reedy outset; it enforces contemplation.
We arrive. We traverse depth in thudding silence. We go on.

Little Boy Impelling a Scooter

Little boy on a wet pavement
near nightfall, balancing his scooter,
his free foot spurring it along,
his every speeding touchdown
striking a match of spent light,
the long concrete patched with squeezed-dry impacts
coming and going, his tyres' rubber edge
splitting the fine water. He jinks the handlebars
and trots around them, turning them
back, and stamps fresh small impulsions
maddeningly on and near, off and behind
his earlier impulses.
                    Void blurring pavement stars,
void blurring wheel-noise, uneven with hemmed outsets
as the dark deepens over town. To bear his rapture,
to smile, to share in it, require attitudes
all remote from murder,
watching his bowed intent face and slackly trailing
sudden pump leg passing and hemm! repassing
under powerlines and windy leaves
and the bared night sky's interminable splendours.

The Hypogeum

Below the moveable gardens of this shopping centre
down concrete ways
                        to a level of rainwater,
a black lake glimmering among piers, electric lighted,
windless, of no depth.
                        Rare shafts of daylight
waver at their base. As the water is shaken, the few
cars parked down here seem to rock. In everything
there strains that silent crash, that reverberation
which persists in concrete.
                        The cardboard carton
Lorenzo's Natural Flavour Italian Meat Balls has foundered
into a wet ruin. Dutch Cleanser is propped at a high
featureless wall. Self-raising Flour is still floating
and supermarket trolleys hang their inverse harps,
silver leaking from them.
                        What will help the informally religious
to endure peace? Surface water dripping into
this underworld makes now a musical blip,
now rings from nowhere.
                        Young people descending the ramp
pause at the water's brink, banging their voices.

Second Essay on Interest: The Emu

Weathered blond as a grass tree, a huge Beatles haircut
raises an alert periscope and stares out
over scrub. Her large olivine eggs click
oilily together; her lips of noble plastic
clamped in their expression, her head-fluff a stripe
worn mohawk style, she bubbles her pale-blue windpipe:
the emu, *Dromaius novaehollandiae*,
whose stand-in on most continents is an antelope,
looks us in both eyes with her one eye
and her other eye, dignified courageous hump,
feather-swaying condensed camel, Swift Courser of New Holland.

Knees backward in toothed three-way boots, you stand,
Dinewan, proud emu, common as the dust
in your sleeveless cloak, returning our interest.
Your shield of fashion's wobbly: you're Quaint, you're Native,
even somewhat Bygone. You may be let live
but beware: the blank zones of Serious disdain
are often carte blanche to the darkly human.
Europe's boats on their first strange shore looked humble
but, Mass over, men started renaming the creatures.
Worship turned to interest and had new features.
Now only life survives, if it's made remarkable.

Heraldic bird, our protection is a fable
made of space and neglect. We're remarkable and not;
we're the ordinary discovered on a strange planet.
Are you Early or Late, in the history of birds
which doesn't exist, and is deeply ancient?
My kinships, too, are immemorial and recent,
like my country, which abstracts yours in words.
This distillate of mountains is finely branched, this plain
expanse of dour delicate lives, where the rain,
shrouded slab on the west horizon, is a corrugated revenant
settling its long clay-tipped plumage in a hatching descent.

Rubberneck, stepped sister, I see your eye on our jeep's load.
I think your story is, when you were offered

the hand of evolution, you gulped it. Forefinger and thumb
project from your face, but the weighing palm is inside you
collecting the bottletops, nails, wet cement that you famously
    swallow,
your passing muffled show, your serially private museum.
Some truths are now called *trivial,* though. Only God approves
    them.
Some humans who disdain them make a kind of weather
which, when it grows overt and widespread, we call *war.*
There we make death trivial and awesome, by rapid turns about,
we conscript it to bless us, force-feed it to squeeze the drama out;

indeed we imprison and torture death—this part is called *peace*—
we offer it murder like mendicants, begging for significance.
You rustle dreams of pardon, not fleeing in your hovercraft style,
not gliding fast with zinc-flaked legs dangling, feet making high-
    tensile
seesawing impacts. Wasteland parent, barely edible dignitary,
the disinterested spotlight of the lords of interest
and gowned nobles of ennui is a torch of vivid arrest
and blinding after-darkness. But you hint it's a brigand sovereignty
after the steady extents of God's common immortality
whose image is daylight detail, aggregate, in process yet plumb
to the everywhere focus of one devoid of boredom.

A Retrospect of Humidity

All the air conditioners now slacken
their hummed carrier wave. Once again
we've served our three months with remissions
in the steam and dry iron of this seaboard.
In jellied glare, through the nettle-rash season,
we've watched the sky's fermenting laundry
portend downpours. Some came, and steamed away,
and we were clutched back into the rancid
saline midnights of orifice weather,
to damp grittiness and wiping off the air.

Metaphors slump irritably together in
the muggy weeks. Shark and jellyfish shallows
become suburbs where you breathe a fat towel;
babies burst like tomatoes with discomfort
in the cotton-wrapped pointing street markets;
the lycra-bulging surf drips from non-swimmers
miles from shore, and somehow includes soil.
Skins, touching, soak each other. Skin touching
any surface wets that and itself
in a kind of mutual digestion.
Throbbing heads grow lianas of nonsense.

It's our annual visit to the latitudes
of rice, kerosene and resignation,
an averted, temporary visit
unrelated, for most, to the attitudes
of festive northbound jets gaining height—
closer, for some few, to the memory
of ulcers scraped with a tin spoon
or sweated faces bowing before dry
where the flesh is worn inside out,
all the hunger-organs clutched in rank nylon,
by those for whom exhaustion is spirit:

an intrusive, heart-narrowing season
at this far southern foot of the monsoon.

As the kleenex flower, the hibiscus
drops its browning wads, we forget
annually, as one forgets a sickness.
The stifling days will never come again,
not now that we've seen the first sweater
tugged down on the beauties of division
and inside the rain's millions, a risen
loaf of cat on a cool night verandah.

Flowering Eucalypt in Autumn

That slim creek out of the sky
the dried-blood western gum tree
is all stir in its high reaches:

its strung haze-blue foliage is dancing
points down in breezy mobs, swapping
pace and place in an all-over sway

retarded en masse by crimson blossom.
Bees still at work up there tack
around their exploded furry likeness

and the lawn underneath's a napped rug
of eyelash drift, of blooms flared
like a sneeze in a redhaired nostril,

minute urns, pinch-sized rockets
knocked down by winds, by night-creaking
fig-squirting bats, or the daily

parrot gang with green pocketknife wings.
Bristling food for tough delicate
raucous life, each flower comes

as a spray in its own turned vase,
a taut starburst, honeyed model
of the tree's fragrance crisping in your head.

When the Japanese plum tree
was shedding in spring, we speculated
there among the drizzling petals

what kind of exquisitely precious
artistic bloom might be gendered
in a pure ethereal compost

of petals potted as they fell.
From unpetalled gum–debris
we know what is grown continually,

a tower of fabulous swish tatters,
a map hoisted upright, a crusted
riverbed with up–country show towns.

The Chimes of Neverwhere

How many times did the Church prevent war?
Who knows? Those wars did not occur.
How many numbers don't count before ten?
Treasures of the Devil in Neverwhere.

The neither state of Neverwhere
is hard to place as near or far
since all things that didn't take place are there
and things that have lost the place they took:

Herr Hitler's buildings, King James' cigar,
the happiness of Armenia,
the Abelard children, the Manchus' return
are there with the Pictish Grammar Book.

The girl who returned your dazzled look
and the mornings you might have woke to her
are your waterbed in Neverwhere.
There shine the dukes of Australia

and all the great poems that never were
quite written, and every balked invention.
There too are the Third AIF and its war
in which I and boys my age were killed

more pointlessly with each passing year.
There too half the works of sainthood are
the enslavements, tortures, rapes, despair
deflected by them from the actual

to beat on the human-sacrifice drum
that billions need not die to hear
since Christ's love of them struck it dumb
and his agony keeps it in Neverwhere.

How many times did the Church bring peace?
More times than it happened. Leave it back there:
the children we didn't let out of there need it,
for the Devil's at home in Neverwhere.

The Smell of Coal Smoke

John Brown, glowing far and down,
wartime Newcastle was a brown town,
handrolled cough and cardigan, rain on paving bricks,
big smoke to a four-year-old from the green sticks.
Train city, mother's city, coming on dark,
Japanese shell holes awesome in a park,
electric light and upstairs, encountered first that day,
sailors and funny ladies in Jerry's Fish Café.

It is always evening on those earliest trips,
raining through the tram wires where blue glare rips
across the gaze of wonderment and leaves thrilling tips.
The steelworks' vast roofed débris unrolling falls
of smoky stunning orange, its eye-hurting slump walls
mellow to lounge interiors, cut pile and curry-brown
with the Pears-Soap-smelling fire and a sense of ships
mourning to each other below in the town.

This was my mother's childhood and her difference,
her city-brisk relations who valued Sense
talking strike and colliery, engineering, fowls and war,
Brown's grit and miners breathing it, years before
as I sat near the fire, raptly touching coal,
its blockage, slick yet dusty, prisms massed and dense
in the iron scuttle, its hammered bulky roll
into the glaring grate to fracture and shoal,

its chips you couldn't draw with on the cement
made it a stone, tar crockery, different—
and I had three grandparents, while others had four:
where was my mother's father, never called Poor?
In his tie and his Vauxhall that had a boat bow
driving up the Coalfields, but where was he now?
Coal smoke as much as gum trees now had a tight scent
to summon deep brown evenings of the Japanese war,

to conjure gaslit pub yards, their razory frisson
and sense my dead grandfather, the Grafton Cornishman,

rising through the night schools by the pressure in his chest
as his lungs creaked like mahogany with the grains of John Brown.
His city, mother's city, at its starriest
as swearing men with doctors' bags streamed by toward the docks
past the smoke-frothing wooden train that would take us home
    soon
with our day-old Henholme chickens peeping in their box.

Time Travel

To revisit the spitfire world
of the duel, you put on a suit
of white body armour, a helmet
like an insect's composite eye
and step out like a space walker
under haloed lights, trailing a cord.

Descending, with nodding foil in hand
towards the pomander-and-cravat sphere
you meet the Opponent, for this journey
can only be accomplished by a pair
who semaphore and swap quick respect
before they set about their joint effect

which is making zeroes and serifs so
swiftly and with such sprung variety
that the long steels skid, clatter, zing,
switch, batter, bite, kiss and ring
in the complex rhythms of that society
with its warrior snare of comme il faut

that has you facing a starched beau
near stable walls on a misty morning,
striking, seeking the surrender in him,
the pedigree-flaw through which to pin him,
he probing for your own braggadocio,
confusion, ennui or inner fawning—

Seconds, holding stakes and cloths, look grim
and surge a step. Exchanges halt
for one of you stands, ageing horribly,
collapses, drowning from an entry
of narrow hurt. The other gulps hot chocolate
a trifle fast, but talking nonchalant—

a buzzer sounds. Heads are tucked
under arms, and you and he swap
curt nods in a more Christian century.

Late Snow in Edinburgh

Snow on the day before Anzac!
A lamb-killing wind out of Ayr
heaped a cloud up on towering Edinburgh
in the night, and left it adhering
to parks and leafing trees in the morning,
a cloud decaying on the upper city,
on the stepped medieval skyscrapers there,
cassata broadcast on the lower city
to be a hiss on buzzing cobblestones
under soaped cars, and cars still shaving.

All day the multiplying whiteness
persisted, now dazzling, now resumed
into the spectral Northern weather,
moist curd out along the Castle clifftops,
linen collar on the Mound, pristine pickings
in the Cowgate's blackened teeth, deposits
in Sir Walter Scott's worked tusk, and under
the soaked blue banners walling Princes Street.
The lunchtime gun fired across dun distances
ragged with keen tents. By afternoon, though,
derelicts sleeping immaculate in wynds
and black areas had shrivelled to wet sheep.
Froth, fading, stretched thinner on allotments.

As the melting air browned into evening
the photographed city, in last umber
and misty first lights, was turning into
the stones in a vast furrow. For that moment
half a million moved in an earth cloud
harrowed up, damp and fuming, seeded
with starry points, with luminous still patches
that wouldn't last the night. No Anzac Day
prodigies for the visitor-descendant.
The snow was dimming into Spring's old
Flanders jacket and frieze trousers. Hughie Spring,
the droll ploughman, up from the Borders.

■ Flood Plains on the Coast Facing Asia

Hitching blur to a caged propeller
with its motor racket swelling
barroom to barrage, our aluminium
airboat has crossed the black coffee
lagoon and swum out onto
one enormous crinkling green.
Now like a rocket loudening
to liftoff, it erects the earsplitting
wigwam we must travel in
everywhere here, and starts skimming
at speed on the never-never
meadows of the monsoon wetland.

Birds lift, scattering before us
over the primeval irrigation,
leaf-running jacanas, twin-boomed
with supplicant bare feet for tails;
knob-headed magpie geese
row into the air ahead of us;
waterlilies lean away, to go
under as we overrun them
and resurrect behind us.
We leave at most a darker green
trace on the universal glittering
and, waterproof in cream and blue,
waterlilies on their stems, circling.

Our shattering car
crossing exposed and seeping spaces
brings us to finely stinking places,
yet whatever riceless paddies
we reach, of whatever grass,
there is always sheeting spray
underhull for our passage;
and the Intermediate Egret leaps
aloft out of stagnant colours
and many a double-barrelled crossbow

shoots vegetable breath emphatically
from the haunts of flaking buffalo;
water glinting everywhere, like ice,
we traverse speeds humans once reached
in such surroundings mainly
as soldiers, in the tropic wars.

At times, we fold our windtunnel
away, in its blackened steel sail
and sit, for talk and contemplation.
For instance, off the deadly islet,
a swamp-surrounded sandstone knoll
split, cabled, commissured
with fig trees' python roots.
Watched by distant plateau cliffs
stitched millennially in every crevice
with the bark-entubed dead
we do not go ashore.
Those hills are ancient stone gods
just beginning to be literature.

We release again the warring sound
of our peaceful tour, and go sledding
headlong through mounded paperbark
copses, on reaches of maroon
grit, our wake unravelling
over green curd where logs lie digesting
and over the breast-lifting deeps
of the file snake, whom the women here
tread on, scoop up, clamp head-first in their teeth
and jerk to death, then carry home as meat.

Loudest without speech, we shear
for miles on the paddock of nymphaeas
still hoisting up the paired pied geese,
their black goslings toddling below them.
We, a family with baby and two friends,
one swift metal skin above the food-chains,
the extensible wet life-chains of which
our civility and wake are one stretch,

the pelicans circling over us another
and the cat-napping peace of the secure,
of eagles, lions and two-year-old George
asleep beneath his pink linen hat as
we enter domains of flowering lotus.

In our propeller's stiffened silence
we stand up among scalloped leaves
that are flickering for hundreds of acres
on their deeper water. The lotus
prove a breezy nonhuman gathering
of this planet, with their olive-studded
rubbery cocktail glasses, loose carmine roses,
salmon buds like the five-fingertips-joined
gesture of summation, of *ecco!*
waist-high around us in all their greenery
on yeasty frog water. We receive this
sidelong, speaking our wiry language
in which so many others ghost and flicker.

We discuss Leichhardt's party and their qualities
when, hauling the year 1845
through here, with spearheads embedded in it,
their bullock drays reached and began skirting
this bar of literal water
after the desert months which had been
themselves a kind of swimming,
a salt undersea plodding, monster-haunted
with odd very pure surfacings.
We also receive, in drifts of calm
hushing, which fret the baby boy,
how the fuzzed gold innumerable cables
by which this garden hangs skyward
branch beneath the surface, like dreams.

The powerful dream of being harmless,
the many chains snapped and stretched hard for that:
both shimmer behind our run back
toward the escarpments where stallion-eyed
Lightning lives, who'd shiver all heights

down and make of the earth
one oozing, feeding peneplain.
Unprotected Lightning: there are his wild horses
and brolgas, and far heron not rising.
Suddenly we run over a crocodile.
On an unlilied deep, bare even
of minute water fern, it leaped out,
surged man-swift straight under us. We ran over it.
We circle back. Unhurt, it floats, peering
from each small eye turret, then annuls
buoyance and merges subtly under,
swollen leathers becoming gargoyle stone,
chains of contour, with pineapple abdomen.

■ The Dream of Wearing Shorts Forever

To go home and wear shorts forever
in the enormous paddocks, in that warm climate,
adding a sweater when winter soaks the grass,

to camp out along the river bends
for good, wearing shorts, with a pocketknife,
a fishing line and matches,

or there where the hills are all down, below the plain,
to sit around in shorts at evening
on the plank verandah—

If the cardinal points of costume
are Robes, Tat, Rig and Scunge,
where are shorts in this compass?

They are never Robes
as other bareleg outfits have been:
the toga, the kilt, the lava-lava
the Mahatma's cotton dhoti;

archbishops and field marshals
at their ceremonies never wear shorts.
The very word
means underpants in North America.

Shorts can be Tat,
Land-Rovering bush-environmental tat,
socio-political ripped-and-metal-stapled tat,
solidarity-with-the-Third-World tat tvam asi,

likewise track-and-field shorts worn to parties
and the further humid, modelling negligée
of the Kingdom of Flaunt,
that unchallenged aristocracy.

More plainly climatic, shorts
are farmers' rig leathery with salt and bonemeal,

are sailors' and branch bankers' rig,
the crisp golfing style
of our youngest male National Costume.

Most loosely, they are Scunge,
ancient Bengal bloomers or moth-eaten hot pants
worn with a former shirt,
feet, beach sand, hair
and a paucity of signals.

Scunge, which is real negligée
housework in a swimsuit, pyjamas worn all day,
is holiday, is freedom from ambition.
Scunge makes you invisible
to the world and yourself.

The entropy of costume,
scunge can get you conquered by more vigorous cultures
and help you to notice it less.

Satisfied ambition, defeat, true unconcern,
the wish and the knack for self-forgetfulness
all fall within the scunge ambit
wearing board shorts or similar;
it is a kind of weightlessness.

Unlike public nakedness, which in Westerners
is deeply circumstantial, relaxed as exam time,
artless and equal as the corsetry of a hussar regiment,

shorts and their plain like
are an angelic nudity,
spirituality with pockets!
A double updraft as you drop from branch to pool!

Ideal for getting served last
in shops of the temperate zone
they are also ideal for going home, into space,
into time, to farm the mind's Sabine acres
for product or subsistence.

Now that everyone who yearned to wear long pants
has essentially achieved them,
long pants, which have themselves been underwear
repeatedly, and underground more than once,
it is time perhaps to cherish the culture of shorts,

to moderate grim vigour
with the knobble of bare knees,
to cool bareknuckle feet in inland water,
slapping flies with a book on solar wind
or a patient bare hand, beneath the cadjiput trees,

to be walking meditatively
among green timber, through the grassy forest
towards a calm sea
and looking across to more of that great island
and the further topics.

■ The Sleepout

Childhood sleeps in a verandah room
in an iron bed close to the wall
where the winter over the railing
swelled the blind on its timber boom

and splinters picked lint off warm linen
and the stars were out over the hill;
then one wall of the room was forest
and all things in there were to come.

Breathings climbed up on the verandah
when dark cattle rubbed at a corner
and sometimes dim towering rain stood
for forest, and the dry cave hunched woollen.

Inside the forest was lamplit
along tracks to a starry creek bed
and beyond lay the never-fenced country,
its full billabongs all surrounded

by animals and birds, in loud crustings,
and something kept leaping up amongst them.
And out there, to kindle whenever
dark found it, hung the daylight moon.

▌ Louvres

In the banana zone, in the poinciana tropics
reality is stacked on handsbreadth shelving,
open and shut, it is ruled across with lines
as in a gleaming gritty exercise book.

The world is seen through a cranked or levered
weatherboarding of explosive glass
angled floor-to-ceiling. Horizons which metre
the dazzling outdoors into green-edged couplets.

In the louvred latitudes
children fly to sleep in triplanes, and
cool nights are eerie with retracting flaps.

Their houses stand aloft among bougainvillea,
covered bridges that lead down a shining hall
from love to mystery to breakfast,
from babyhood to moving-out day

and visitors shimmer up in columnar gauges
to touch lives lived behind gauze
in a lantern of inventory,
slick vector geometries glossing the months of rain.

There, nudity is dizzily cubist, and directions
have to include: stage left, add an inch of breeze
or: enter a glistening tendril.

Every building of jinked and slatted ledges
is at times a squadron of inside-out
helicopters, humming with rotor fans.

For drinkers under cyclonic pressure, such
a house can be a bridge of scythes—
groundlings scuffing by stop only for dénouements.

But everyone comes out on platforms of command
to survey cloudy flame-trees, the plain of streets, the future:
only then descending to the level of affairs

and if these things are done in the green season
what to do in the crystalline dry? Well
below in the struts of laundry is the four-wheel drive

vehicle in which to make an expedition
to the bush, or as we now say the Land,
the three quarters of our continent
set aside for mystic poetry.

The Drugs of War

On vinegar and sour fish sauce Rome's legions stemmed
    avalanches
of whirling golden warriors whose lands furnished veterans'
    ranches;
when the warriors broke through at last, they'd invented sour
    mash
but they took to sugared wines and failed to hold the lands of
    hash.

By beat of drum in the wars of rum flogged peasant boys faced
    front
and their warrior chiefs conversed coolly, attired for the hunt,
and tobacco came in, in a pipe of peace, but joined the pipes of
    war
as an after-smoke of battle, or over the maps before.

All alcohols, all spirits lost strength in the trenches, that belt-fed
    country
then morphine summoned warrior dreams in ruined and would-
    be gentry;
stewed tea and vodka and benzedrine helped quell that
    mechanized fury—
the side that won by half a head then provided judge and jury.

In the acid war the word was Score; rising helicopters cried
    Smack! Smack!
Boys laid a napalm trip on earth and tried to take it back
but the pot boiled over in the rear; fighters tripped on their lines
    of force
and victory went to the supple hard side, eaters of fish sauce.

The perennial war drugs are made in ourselves: sex and adrenalin,
blood, and the endomorphias that transmute defeat and pain
and others hardly less chemical: eagles, justice, loyalty, edge,
the Judas face of every idea, and the fish that ferments in the
    brain.

Letters to the Winner

After the war, and just after marriage and fatherhood
ended in divorce, our neighbour won the special lottery,
an amount then equal to fifteen years of a manager's
salary at the bank, or fifty years' earnings by
a marginal farmer fermenting his clothes in the black
marinade of sweat, up in his mill-logging paddocks.

The district, used to one mailbag, now received two
every mailday. The fat one was for our neighbour.
After a dip or two, he let these bags accumulate
around the plank walls of the kitchen, over the chairs,
till on a rainy day, he fed the tail-switching calves,
let the bullocks out of the yard, and, pausing at the door
to wash his hands, came inside to read the letters.

Shaken out in a vast mound on the kitchen table
they slid down, slithered to his fingers. *I have 7 children
I am under the doctor if you could see your way clear
equal Pardners in the Venture God would bless you lovey
assured of our best service for a mere fifteen pounds down
remember you're only lucky I knew you from the paper straightaway*

Baksheesh, hissed the pages as he flattened them, baksheesh!
*mate if your interested in a fellow diggers problems
old mate a friend in need*—the Great Golden Letter
having come, now he was being punished for it.
*You sound like a lovely big boy we could have such times
her's my photoe Doll Im wearing my birthday swimsuit
with the right man I would share this infallible system.*

When he lifted the stove's iron disc and started feeding in
the pages he'd read, they clutched and streamed up the corrugated
black chimney shaft. And yet he went on reading,
holding each page by its points, feeling an obligation
to read each crude rehearsed lie, each come-on, flat truth,
    extremity:
We might visit you the wise investor a loan a bush man like you

remember we met on Roma Street for your delight and mine
a lick of the sultana—the white moraine kept slipping
its messages to him *you will be accursed* he husked them like cobs
Mr Nouveau Jack old man my legs are all paralysed up.
Black smuts swirled weightless in the room *some good kind person*
like the nausea of a novice free-falling in a deep mine's cage
now I have lost his pension and formed a sticky nimbus round him

but he read on, fascinated by a further human range
not even war had taught him, nor literature glossed for him
since he never read literature. Merely the great reject pile
which high style is there to snub and filter, for readers.
That his one day's reading had a strong taste of what he and war
had made of his marriage is likely; he was not without sympathy,

but his leap had hit a wire through which the human is policed.
His head throbbed as if busting with a soundless shout
of immemorial sobbed invective *God-forsaken, God-forsakin*
as he stopped reading, and sat blackened in his riches.

■ The Milk Lorry

Now the milk lorry is a polished submarine
that rolls up at midday, attaches a trunk and inhales
the dairy's tank to a frosty snore in minutes

but its forerunner was the high-tyred barn of crisp mornings,
reeking Diesel and mammary, hazy in its roped interior
as a carpet under beaters, as it crashed along potholed lanes

cooeeing at schoolgirls. Long planks like unshipped oars
butted, levelling in there, because between each farm's
stranded wharf of milk cans, the work was feverish slotting

of floors above floors, for load. It was sling out the bashed
paint-collared empties and waltz in the full,
stumbling on their rims under ribaldry, tilting their big gallons

then the schoolboy's calisthenic, hoisting steel men man-high
till the glancing hold was a magazine of casque armour,
a tinplate 'tween-decks, a seminar engrossed

in one swaying tradition, behind the speeding doorways
that tempted a truant to brace and drop, short of town,
and spend the day, with book or not, down under

the bridge of a river that by dinnertime would be
tongueing like cattledogs, or down a moth-dusty reach
where the fish-feeding milk boat and cedar barge once floated.

The Butter Factory

It was built of things that must not mix:
paint, cream and water, fire and dusty oil.
You heard the water dreaming in its large
kneed pipes, up from the weir. And the cordwood
our fathers cut for the furnace stood in walls
like the sleeper-stacks of a continental railway.

The cream arrived in lorried tides; its procession
crossed a platform of workers' stagecraft: *Come here
Friday-Legs! Or I'll feel your hernia—*
Overalled in milk's colour, men moved the heart of milk,
separated into thousands, along a roller track—*Trucks?
That one of mine, son, it pulls like a sixteen-year-old—*
to the tester who broached the can lids, causing fat tears,
who tasted, dipped and did his thin stoppered chemistry
on our labour, as the empties chattered downstage and fumed.

Under the high roof, black-crusted and stainless steels
were walled apart: black romped with leather belts
but paddlewheels sailed the silvery vats where muscles
of the one deep cream were exercised to a bullion
to be blocked in paper. And between waves of delivery
the men trod on water, hosing the rainbows of a shift.

It was damp April even at Christmas round every
margin of the factory. Also it opened the mouth
to see tackles on glibbed gravel, and the mossed char louvres
of the ice-plant's timber tower streaming with
heavy rain all day, above the droughty paddocks
of the totem cows round whom our lives were dancing.

Bats' Ultrasound

Sleeping-bagged in a duplex wing
with fleas, in rock-cleft or building
radar bats are darkness in miniature,
their whole face one tufty crinkled ear
with weak eyes, fine teeth bared to sing.

Few are vampires. None flit through the mirror.
Where they flutter at evening's a queer
tonal hunting zone above highest C.
Insect prey at the peak of our hearing
drone re to their detailing tee:

ah, eyrie-ire, aero hour, eh?
O'er our ur-area (our era aye
ere your raw row) we air our array,
err, yaw, row wry—aura our orrery,
our eerie ü our ray, our arrow.

A rare ear, our aery Yahweh.

The Lake Surnames

There are rental houseboats down the lakes now.
Two people facing, with drinks, in a restaurant party
talk about them: *That idiot, he ran us aground*
in the dark! These fishermen rescued us,
towed us off the mudbank. They were frightening actually,
real inbred faces, Deliverance people
when we saw them by torchlight in their boat—

> For an instant, rain rattles at the glass
> and brown cardboards of a kitchen window
> and drips lamplight-coloured out of soot
> in the fireplace, hitching steam off stove-iron.

> Tins of beeswax, nails and poultice mixture
> stick to shelves behind the door. Triangular
> too, the caramel dark up under rafters
> is shared, above one plank wall, by the room

> where the English housekeeper screamed
> at a crisp bat on the lino. Guest room,
> parents' room, always called *the room*
> with tennis racquet and rifle in the lowboy.

> Quick steps jingle the glassed cabinet
> as a figure fishes spoons from scalding water
> ("what's not clean's sterilised") in the board-railed
> double triangle of a kerosene-tin sink,

> a real Bogan sink, on the table.
> The upright wireless, having died when valves vanished,
> has its back to the wall. It is a *plant* for money
> guarded by a nesting snake, who'll be killed when discovered.

> The new car outside, streaming cricket scores,
> is a sit-in radio, glowing, tightly furnished
> but in the Auburn wood stove, the fire laps
> and is luxury too, in one of them flood years.

—With only the briefest pause, the other
answers: *There aren't that many full-time
surnames down the lakes. If you'd addressed them
as Mr Blanche, Mr Woodward, Mr Legge,
Mr Bramble, or Palmer, your own surname,
you'd probably have been right. And more at ease.*

Nocturne

Brisbane, night-gathered, far away
estuarine imaginary city
of houses towering down one side
of slatted lights seen under leaves

confluence of ranginess with lush,
Brisbane, of rotogravure memory
approached by web lines of coke and grit
by sleepers racked in corridor trains

weatherboard incantatory city
of the timber duchess, the strapped port
in Auchenflower and Fortitude Valley
and bottletops spat in Vulture Street

greatest of the floodtime towns
that choked the dictionary with silt
and hung a navy in the tropic gardens.
Brisbane, on the steep green slope to war

brothel-humid headquarters city
where commandos and their allies fought
down café stairs, belt buckle and boot
and once with a rattletrap green gun.

In midnight nets, in mango bombings
Brisbane, storied and cable-fixed,
above your rum river, farewell and adieu
in marble on the hill of Toowong

by golfing pockets, by deep squared pockets
night heals the bubbled tar of day
and the crab moon, rising, reddens above
Brisbane, rotating far away.

Lotus Dam

Lotus leaves, standing feet above the water,
collect at their centre a perfect lens of rain
and heel, and tip it back into the water.

Their baby leaves are feet again, or slant lips
scrolled in declaration; pointed at toe and heel
they echo an unwalked sole in their pale green crinkles

and under blown and picket blooms, the floor
of floating leaves rolls light rainwater marbles
back and forth on sharkskins of anchored rippling.

Each speculum, pearl and pebble of the first water
rides, sprung with weight, on its live mirroring skin
tipped green and loganberry, till one or other sky

redeems it, beneath bent foils and ferruled canes
where cupped pink bursts all day, above riddled water.

Hearing Impairment

Hearing loss? Yes, loss is what we hear
who are starting to go deaf. Loss
trails a lot of weird puns in its wake, viz.
Dad's a real prism of the Left—
you'd like me to repeat that?
THE SAD SURREALISM OF THE DEAF.

It's mind over mutter at work
guessing half what the munglers are saying
and society's worse. Punchlines elude to you
as Henry Lawson and other touchy drinkers
have claimed. Asides, too, go pasture.
It's particularly nasty with a wether.

First you crane at people, face them
while you can still face them. But grudgually
you give up dinnier parties; you begin
to think about Beethoven; you Hanover
next visit here on silly Narda Fearing—I SAY
YOU CAN HAVE AN EXQUISITE EAR
AND STILL BE HARD OF HEARING.

It seems to be mainly speech, at first,
that escapes you—and that can be a rest,
the poor man's escape itch from Babel.
You can still hear a duck way upriver,
a lorry miles off on the highway. You
can still say boo to a goose and
read its curt yellow-lipped reply.
You can shout SING UP to a magpie,

but one day soon you must feel
the silent stopwatch chill your ear
in the doctor's rooms, and be wired
back into a slightly thinned world
with a faint plastic undertone to it
and, if the rumours are true, snatches

of static, music, police transmissions:
it's a BARF minor Car Fourteen prospect.

But maybe hearing aids are now perfect
and maybe it's not all that soon.
Sweet nothings in your ear are still sweet;
you've heard the human range by your age
and can follow most talk from memory;
the peace of the graveyard's well up
on that of the grave. And the world would
enjoy peace and birdsong for more moments

if you were head of government, enquiring
of an aide Why, Simpkins, do you tell me
a warrior is a ready flirt?
I might argue—and flowers keep blooming
as he swallows his larynx to shriek
our common mind-overloading sentence:
I'M SORRY, SIR, IT'S A RED ALERT!

Poetry and Religion

Religions are poems. They concert
our daylight and dreaming mind, our
emotions, instinct, breath and native gesture

into the only whole thinking: poetry.
Nothing's said till it's dreamed out in words
and nothing's true that figures in words only.

A poem, compared with an arrayed religion,
may be like a soldier's one short marriage night
to die and live by. But that is a small religion.

Full religion is the large poem in loving repetition;
like any poem, it must be inexhaustible and complete
with turns where we ask Now why did the poet do that?

You can't pray a lie, said Huckleberry Finn;
you can't poe one either. It is the same mirror:
mobile, glancing, we call it poetry,

fixed centrally, we call it a religion,
and God is the poetry caught in any religion,
caught, not imprisoned. Caught as in a mirror

that he attracted, being in the world as poetry
is in the poem, a law against its closure.
There'll always be religion around while there is poetry

or a lack of it. Both are given, and intermittent,
as the action of those birds—crested pigeon, rosella parrot—
who fly with wings shut, then beating, and again shut.

When Bounty Is Down
to Persimmons and Lemons

(from "The Idyll Wheel")

In May, Mary's month,
when snakes go to sleep,
sunlight and shade lengthen,
forest grows deep,

wood coughs at the axe
and splinters hurt worse,
barbed wire pulls through
every post in reverse,

old horses grow shaggy
and flies hunker down
on curtains, like sequins
on a dead girl's ball gown.

Grey soldier-birds arrive
in flickers of speed
to hang upside down
from a quivering weed

or tremble trees' foliage
that they trickle down through.
Women's Weekly summer fashions
in the compost turn blue.

The sun slants in under things
and stares right through houses;
soon pyjamas will peep, though,
from the bottoms of trousers.

Night-barking dogs quieten
as overcast forms
and it rains, with far thunder,
in queer predawn storms;

then the school bus tops ridges
with clay marks for effort,
picking up drowsy schoolkids,
none of them now barefoot,

and farmers take spanners
to the balers, gang ploughs
and towering diesel tractors
they prefer to their cows.

The Kitchens

(from "The Idyll Wheel")

This deep in the year, in the frosts of then
that steeled sheets left ghostly on the stayed line,
smoked over verandah beds, cruelled water taps rigid,
family and visitors would sit beside the lake
of blinding coals, that end of the detached kitchen,
the older fellows quoting qoph *and* resh
from the Book of Psalms, as they sizzled phlegm
(some still did it after iron stoves came
and the young moved off to cards and the radio)
and all told stories. That's a kind of spoken video:

We rode through from the Myall
on that road of the cedarcutter's ghost.
All this was called Wild Horses Creek then;
you could plait the grass over the pommel
of your saddle. That grass don't grow now.
I remember we camped on Waterloo that night
there where the black men gave the troopers a hiding.

The garden was all she had: the parrots were at it
and she came out and said to them, quite serious
like as if to reasonable people They are *my* peas.
And do you know? They flew off and never come back.

If you missed anything: plough,
saddle, cornplanter, shovel,
you just went across to Uncle Bob's
and brought it home. If he
was there, he never looked ashamed:
he'd just tell you a joke,
some lies, sing you a poem,
keep you there drinking all night—

Bloody cruel mongrels, telling me the native bear
would grow a new hide if you skun it alive.

Everybody knows that, they told me. I told them
if I caught any man skinning bears alive
on my place, he'd bloody need a new hide himself.

    Tommy Turpin the blackfellow said to me More better
    you walk behind me today, eh boss.
    Might be devil-devil tell me hit you with the axe
    longa back of the head. I thought he was joking
    then I saw he wasn't. My word I stayed behind
    that day, with the axe, trimming tongues on the rails
    while he cut mortises out of the posts. I listened.

I wis eight year old, an Faither gied me the lang gun
tae gang doon an shuit the native hens at wis aitin
aa oor oats. I reasoned gin ye pit ae chairge
i the gun, pouder waddin an shot, ye got ae shot
sae pit in twa, ye'd get twa. Aweel, I pit in seven,
liggd doon ahint a stump, pu'd the trigger—an the warld
gaed milky white. I think I visited Scotland
whaur I had never been. It was a ferlie I wis seean.
It wis a sonsy place. But Grannie gard me gang back.
Mither wis skailan watter on ma heid, greetin. As they found
o the gun wis stump-flinders, but there wis a black scour thro the
    oats,
an unco ringan in ma ears, an fifteen deid native hens.

    Of course long tongue she laughed about that other
    and they pumped her about you can guess and hanging round
      there
    and she said He's got one on him like a horse, Mama,
    and I like it. Well! And all because of you know—

Father couldn't stand meanness.
When Uncle you-know-who
charged money for milking our cows
that time Isabel took bad
Father called him gutless,
not just tin-arsed, but gutless.
Meanness is for cowards, Father reckoned.

The little devil, he says to the minister's wife
Daddy reckons we can't have any more children,
we need the milk for the pigs. Dear I was mortified—

Poor Auntie Mary was dying Old and frail
all scroopered down in the bedclothes pale as cotton
even her hardworking old hands Oh it was sad
people in the room her big daughters performing
rattling the bedknobs There is a white angel
in the room says Mary in this weird voice And then
NO! she heaves herself up Bloody no! Be quiet!
she coughed and spat Phoo! I'll be damned if I'll die!
She's back making bread next week Lived ten more years.

Well, it was black Navy rum; it buggered Darcy.
Fell off his horse, crawled under the cemetery fence.
Then some yahoos cantered past Yez all asleep in there?
All but me, croaks Darcy. They off at a hand gallop,
squealing out, and his horse behind them, stirrups belting it.

The worst ghost I ever saw
was a policeman and (one of the squatters)
moving cattle at night.
I caught them in my headlights.
It haunted me. Every time
I went in to town after that
somehow I'd get arrested—

I'll swear snakes have got no brains!
The carpet snake we had in the rafters
to eat rats, one day it et a chook.
I killed it with the pitchfork, ran a tine
through the top of its head, and chucked it
down the gully. It was back in a week
with a scab on its head and another under its chin.
They bring a house good luck but they got no brain.

Then someone might cup his hand short of the tongue
of a taut violin, try each string to be wrung
by the bow, that spanned razor of holy white hair

and launch all but his earthly weight into an air
that breathed up hearth fires strung worldwide between
the rung hills of being and the pearled hills of been.
In the language beyond speaking they'd sum the grim law,
speed it to a daedaly and foot it to a draw,
the tones of their scale five gnarled fingers wide
and what sang were all angles between love and pride.

▌Midwinter Haircut

(from "The Idyll Wheel")

Now the world has stopped. Dead middle of the year.
Cloud all the colours of a worn-out dairy bucket
freeze-frames the whole sky. The only sun is down
intensely deep in the dam's bewhiskered mirror
and the white-faced heron hides in the drain with her spear.

Now the world has stopped, doors could be left open.
Only one fly came awake to the kitchen heater
this breakfast time, and supped on a rice bubble sluggishly.
No more will come inside out of the frost-crimped grass now.
Crime, too, sits in faraway cars. Phone lines drop at the horizon.

Now the world has stopped, what do we feel like doing?
The district's former haircutter, from the time before barbers, has
        shaved
and wants a haircut. So do I. No longer the munching hand
        clippers
with locks in their gears, nor the scissors more pointed than a
        beak
but the buzzing electric clipper, straight from its cardboard giftbox.

We'll sit under that on the broad-bottomed stool that was
the seat for fifty years of the district's only sit-down job,
the postmistress-telephonist's seat, where our poor great-aunt
who trundled and spoke in sour verdicts sat to hand-crank
the tingling exchange, plugged us into each other's lives

and tapped consolation from gossip's cells as they unlidded.
From her shrewd kind successor who never tapped in, and planes
along below the eaves of our heads, we'll hear a tapestry
of weddings funerals surgeries, and after our sittings
be given a jar of pickle. Hers won't be like the house

a mile down the creek, where cards are cut and shuffled
in the middle of the day, and mortarbombs of beer
detonate the digestion, and they tell world-stopping yarns
like: I went to Sydney races. There along the rails,
  all snap brims and cold eyes, flanked by senior police

  and other, stony men with their eyes in a single crease
  stood the entire Government of New South Wales
  watching Darby ply the whip, all for show, over this fast colt.
  It was young and naïve. It was heading for the post in a bolt
  while the filly carrying his and all the inside money

  strained to come level. Too quick for the stewards to note him
  Darby slipped the colt a low lash to the scrotum.
  It checked, shocked, stumbled—and the filly flashed by.
  As he came from weighing in, I caught Darby's eye
  and he said *Get out of it, mug*, quite conversationally.—

The Misery Cord

(from "The Idyll Wheel")

In Memory of F. S. Murray

Misericord. The Misery Cord.
It was lettered on a wall.
I knew that cord, how it's tough to break
however hard you haul.

My cousin sharefarmed, and so got half:
half dignity, half hope, half income,
for his full work. To get a place
of his own took his whole lifetime.

Some pluck the misery chord from habit
or for luck, however they feel,
some to deceive, and some for the tune—
but sometimes it's real.

Milking bails, flannel shirts, fried breakfasts,
these were our element,
and doubling on horses, and shouting Score!
at a dog yelping on a hot scent—

but an ambulance racing on our back road
is bad news for us all:
the house of community is about
to lose a plank from its wall.

Grief is nothing you can do, but do,
worst work for least reward,
pulling your heart out through your eyes
with tugs of the misery cord.

I looked at my cousin's farm, where he'd just
built his family a house of their own,
and I looked down into Fred's next house,
its clay walls of bluish maroon.

Just one man has broken the misery cord
and lived. He said once was enough.
A poem is an afterlife on earth:
Christ grant us the other half.

DECEMBER

Infant Among Cattle

(from "The Idyll Wheel")

Young parents, up at dawn, working. Their first child can't
be his own babysitter, so as they machine the orphaned milk
from their cows, he must sit plump on the dairy cement,
the back of his keyhole pants safetypinned to a stocking

that is tied to a bench leg. He studies a splotch of cream,
how the bubbles in it, too thick to break, work like
the coated and lucid gravels in the floor. On which he then dings
a steel thing, for the tingling in it and his fingers

till it skips beyond his tether. As the milkers front up
in their heel-less skiddy shoes, he hangs out aslant
on his static line, watching the breeching rope brace them
and their washed udders relieved of the bloodberry ticks

that pull off a stain, and show a calyx of kicking filaments.
By now the light stands up behind the trees like sheet iron.
It photographs the cowyard and dairy-and-bails in one vast
buttery shadow wheel on the trampled junction of paddocks

where the soil is itself a concrete, of dust and seedy stones
and manure crustings. When his father slings a bucketful
of wash water out the door, it wallops and skids
and is gulped down by a sudden maw like the cloth of a radio.

Out and on out, the earth tightens down on the earth
and squeezes heat up through the yellowing grass
like a surfaceless fluid, to pool on open country,
to drip from faces, and breed the insect gleams of midday.

Under the bench, crooning this without words to his rag dog,
he hears a vague trotting outside increase—and the bull
erupts, aghast, through the doorway, dribbling, clay in his curls,
a slit orange tongue working in and out under his belly—

and is repulsed, with buckets and screams and a shovel.
The little boy, swept up in his parents' distress, howls then
but not in fear of the bull, who seemed a sad apparition:
a huge prostrate man, bewildered by a pitiless urgency.

Feb

(from "The Idyll Wheel")

Seedy drytime Feb,
lightning between its teeth,
all its plants pot-bound.

Inside enamelled rims
dams shrink their mirroring shields,
baking the waterlilies.

Days stacked like clay pigeons
squeezed from dust and sweat.
Two cultures: sun and shade.

Days dazed with actuality
like a bottle shot
sniping fruit off twigs,

by afternoon, portentous
with whole cloud-Atlantics
that rain fifteen drops.

Beetroot and iron butter,
bread staled by the fan,
cold chook: that's lunch with Feb.

Weedy drymouth Feb, first cousin of scorched creek stones,
of barbed wire across gaunt gullies, bringer of soldered
death-freckles to the backs of farmers' hands. The mite-struck

foal rattles her itch on fence wires, like her mother,
and scraped hill pastures are grazed back to their charred
bulldozer stitchings. Dogs nip themselves under the tractor

of needy Feb, who waits for the raw eel-perfume
of the first real rain's pheromones, the magic rain-on-dust
sexual scent of Time itself, philtre of all native beings—

Lanky cornhusk Feb,
drilling the red-faced
battalions of tomatoes

through the grader's slots:
harvest out of bareness,
that semidesert mode.

Worn grasshopper month
suddenly void of children;
days tucking their tips in

with blackberry seeds to spit
and all of life root-bound;
stringy dryland Feb.

The Transposition of Clermont

After the Big Flood, we elected
to move our small timber city
from the dangerous beauty of the river
and its fringed lagoons
since both had risen to destroy us.

Many buildings went stacked on wagons
but more were towed entire
in strained stateliness, with a long groyning sound,
up timber by traction engines.

Each moved singly. Life went on round them;
in them, at points of rest.
Guests at breakfast in the Royal Hotel, facing
now the saddlery, now the Town Hall.

We drank in the canted Freemasons
and the progressive Shamrock, but really
all pubs were the Exchange. Relativities
interchanged our world like a chess game:

butcher occluded baker, the police
eclipsed both brothels, the dance hall
sashayed around the Temperance Hall,
front doors sniffed rear, and thoughtfully ground on.

Certain houses burst, and vanished.
One wept its windows, one trailed mementoes up the street.
A taut chain suddenly parted and scythed down
horses and a verandah. Weed-edged black rectangles
in exploded gardens yielded sovereigns and spoons.

That ascent of working architecture
onto the pegged plateau was a children's crusade
with lines stretching down to us.
Everything standing in its wrong accustomed place.
My generation's memories are intricately transposed:

butcher occluding dance music, the police
eclipsed by opportunity, brothels sashaying royally
and, riding sidesaddle up shined skids, the Town Hall.
Excited, we would meet on streets that stayed immutable

sometimes for weeks; from irrecoverable corners
and alleys already widening, we'd look
back down at our new graves and childhood gardens,
the odd house at anchor for a quick tomato season
and the swaying nailed hull of a church going on before us.

And many allotments left unbought, or for expansion
never filled up, above, as they hadn't below.
What was town, what was country stayed elusive
as we saw it always does, in the bush,
what is waste, what is space, what is land.

The Emerald Dove

We ought to hang cutout hawk shapes
in our windows. Birds hard driven
by a predator, or maddened by a mirrored rival
too often die zonk against the panes'
invisible sheer, or stagger away from
the blind full stop in the air.
It was different with the emerald dove.
In at an open sash, a pair

sheered, missile, in a punch of energy,
one jinking on through farther doors, one
thrown, panicked by that rectangular wrong copse, braked
like a bullet in blood, a full-on splat of wings
like a vaulter between shoulders, blazed and calliper,
ashriek out of jagbeaked fixe fury, swatting wind,
lights, keepsakes, panes, then at the in window out, gone.
A sparrowhawk, by the cirrus feathering.

The other, tracked down in a farther room
clinging to a bedhead, was the emerald dove,
a rainforest bird, flashed in beyond its world
of lice, sudden death and tree seeds. Pigeon-like,
only its eye and neck in liquid motion,
there, as much beyond us as beyond
itself, it perched, barefoot in silks
like a prince of Sukhothai, above the reading lamps and cotton-
    buds.

Modest-sized as a writing hand, mushroom fawn
apart from its paua casque, those viridescent closed wings,
it was an emerald Levite in that bedroom
which the memory of it was going to bless for years
despite topping our ordinary happiness, as beauty
makes background of all around it. Levite too
in the question it posed: sanctuary without transformation,
which is, how we might be,

plunged out of our contentment into evolved strange heaven,
where the need to own or mate with or eat the beautiful
was bygone as poverty,
and we were incomprehensibly, in our exhaustion,
treasured, cooed at, then softly left alone
among vast crumples, verticals, refracting air,
our way home barred by mirrors, our splendour unmanifest
to us now, a small wild person, with no idea of peace.

Cave Divers Near Mount Gambier

Chenille-skinned people are counting under the countryside
on resurrections by truck light off among the pines.

Here in the first paddocks, where winter comes ashore,
mild duckweed ponds are skylights of a filled kingdom

and what their gaze absorbs may float up districts away.
White men with scorches of hair approach that water,

zip into black, upturn large flap feet and free-fall
away, their mouths crammed full. Crystalline polyps

of their breathing blossom for a while, as they disturb
algal screens, extinct kangaroos, eels of liquorice colour

then, with the portable greening stars they carry under,
these vanish, as the divers undergo tight anti-births

into the vaults and profound domes of the limestone.
Here, approaching the heart of the poem they embody,

and thereby make the gliding cavern-world embody,
they have to keep time with themselves, and be dull often

with its daylight logic—since to dream it fully
might leave them asprawl on the void clang of their tanks,

their faceplates glazing an unfocussed dreadful portrait
at the apex of a steeple that does not reach the day.

■ The Tin Wash Dish

Lank poverty, dank poverty,
its pants wear through at fork and knee.
It warms its hands over burning shames,
refers to its fate as Them and He
and delights in things by their hard names:
rag and toejam, feed and paw—
don't guts that down, there ain't no more!
Dank poverty, rank poverty,
it hums with a grim fidelity
like wood-rot with a hint of orifice,
wet newspaper jammed in the gaps of artifice,
and disgusts us into fierce loyalty.
It's never the fault of those you love:
poverty comes down from above.
Let it dance chairs and smash the door,
it arises from all that went before
and every outsider's the enemy—
Jesus Christ turned this over with his stick
and knights and philosophers turned it back.
Rank poverty, lank poverty,
chafe in its crotch and sores in its hair,
still a window's clean if it's made of air
and not webbed silver like a sleeve.
Watch out if this does well at school
and has to leave and longs to leave:
someone, sometime, will have to pay.
Lank poverty, dank poverty,
the cornbag quilt breeds such loyalty.
Shave with toilet soap, run to flesh,
astound the nation, run the army,
still you wait for the day you'll be sent back
where books or toys on the floor are rubbish
and no one's allowed to come and play
because home calls itself a shack
and hot water crinkles in the tin wash dish.

The Cows on Killing Day

All me are standing on feed. The sky is shining.

All me have just been milked. Teats all tingling still
from that dry toothless sucking by the chilly mouths
that gasp loudly in in in, and never breathe out.

All me standing on feed, move the feed inside me.
One me smells of needing the bull, that heavy urgent me,
the back-climber, who leaves me humped, straining, but light
and peaceful again, with crystalline moving inside me.

Standing on wet rock, being milked, assuages the calf-sorrow in
    me.
Now the me who needs mounts on me, hopping, to signal the
    bull.

The tractor comes trotting in its grumble; the heifer human
bounces on top of it, and cud comes with the tractor,
big rolls of tight dry feed: lucerne, clovers, buttercup, grass,
that's been bitten but never swallowed, yet is cud.
She walks up over the tractor and down it comes, roll on roll
and all me following, eating it, and dropping the good pats.

The heifer human smells of needing the bull human
and is angry. All me look nervously at her
as she chases the dog me dream of horning dead: our enemy
of the light loose tongue. Me'd jam him in his squeals.

Me, facing every way, spreading out over feed.

One me is still in the yard, the place skinned of feed.
Me, old and sore-boned, little milk in that me now,
licks at the wood. The oldest bull human is coming.

Me in the peed yard. A stick goes out from the human
and cracks, like the whip. Me shivers and falls down
with the terrible, the blood of me, coming out behind an ear.
Me, that other me, down and dreaming in the bare yard.

All me come running. It's like the Hot Part of the sky
that's hard to look at, this that now happens behind wood
in the raw yard. A shining leaf, like off the bitter gum tree
is with the human. It works in the neck of me
and the terrible floods out, swamped and frothy. All me make the
      Roar,
some leaping stiff-kneed, trying to horn that worst horror.
The wolf-at-the-calves is the bull human. Horn the bull human!

But the dog and the heifer human drive away all me.

Looking back, the glistening leaf is still moving.
All of dry old me is crumpled, like the hills of feed,
and a slick me like a huge calf is coming out of me.

The carrion-stinking dog, who is calf of human and wolf,
is chasing and eating little blood things the humans scatter,
and all me run away, over smells, toward the sky.

The Pole Barns

Unchinked log cabins, empty now, or stuffed with hay
under later iron. Or else roofless, bare stanzas of timber
with chars in the text. Each line ends in memorial axemanship.

With a hatch in one gable end, like a cuckoo clock,
they had to be climbed up into, or swung into
from the saddle of a quiet horse, feet-first onto corn.

On logs like rollers these rooms stand on creek flat and ridge,
and their true roofs were bark, every squared sheet a darkened
huge stroke of painting, fibrous from the brush.

Flattened, the sheets strained for a long time to curl again:
the man who slept on one and woke immobilised
in a scroll pipe is a primal pole-barn story.

The sound of rain on bark roofing, dotted, not pointed,
increasing to a sonic blanket, is millennia older than walls
but it was still a heart of storytelling, under the one lantern

as the comets of corn were stripped to their white teeth
and chucked over the partition, and the vellum husks shuffled
    down
round spooky tellers hunched in the planes of winter wind.

More a daylight thinker was the settler who noticed the tide
of his grain going out too fast, and set a dingo trap
in the servery slot—and found his white-faced neighbour,

a man bearded as himself, up to the shoulder in anguish.
Neither spoke as the trap was released, nor mentioned that dawn
    ever.
Happiest, in that iron age, were sitting aloft on the transom

unscrewing corn from cobs, making a good shower for the hens
and sailing the barn, with its log ram jutting low in front.
Like all the ships of conquest, its name was Supply.

The 1812 Overture at Topkapi Saray

The Rosary in Turkish, and prayers for the Sultan.
Through the filigree perforations of a curtain wall
a vagrant breeze parts a hanging mist of muslin
behind the Dowager Wife seated in her pavilion.

For fourteen hundred Sundays she has commended
to the Virgin's Son a fluctuating small congregation
of those who, like herself, had no choice about virginity:
concubines and eunuchs with the faces of aged children.

For perhaps thirteen hundred she has prayed for the Sultan,
both him to whom she was sent as a captured pearl
by the Bey of Algiers, and their son who reigns now in succession
beneath the inscriptions which, though she reads them fluently,
    still

at moments resemble tongues involved with a pastille,
or two, or three. The bitterest to her own taste
was never to succeed in stopping the trade in eunuchs
whereby little boys, never Muslim on the cutting day,

must be seated crying in hot, blood-stanching sand.
A sorrowful mystery. The traffic in bed-girls is another,
but there were eventually also joyous days
when the sea of Martinique yielded to the Marmara's glitter.

Now a messenger approaches the Executioner's House
beyond which only one entire man may pass
into this precinct on the headland of the city,
this Altai meadow of trees and marble tents.

An indifferent face is summoned to the grille
and the letter the messenger brings goes speeding on
to the woman concluding Glory Be among the cushions.
The rest withdraw, rustling, as she reads the superscription:

From the Commander of the Faithful to the Most Illustrious
Lady of the Seraglio—Mother, I have today
made a treaty with the Tsar, ceding one province
and retaining two we had also certainly lost.

These favourable terms arise from the Tsar's great need
of his army to face an invasion by the man Bonaparte,
Commander of the Faithless, to borrow your title for him.
Prospects for the Empire are improved at last

by this invasion, which will come. Russia is very great
but Bonaparte may defeat her. He may be Chinghiz Khan.
Our mightiest enemy would thereby be nullified
and such a victory might well ensnare the victor.

On the other hand, Bonaparte may lose—and then I think
with his legend broken, all Europe would turn on him
with Russia in the van, and engaged in that direction.
I must add, Mother, that as I released the Tsar

for this coming contest, I had in mind our cousin
the Empress Josephine, dear playmate of your childhood
whom the Viper of the Nile so shamefully cast off
two years ago, in his quest for a Habsburg connection.

I was holding an exact balance: the choice was mine
to release the Tsar, or keep him engaged a while longer—
our treacherous Janissaries beat their spoons for this option.
If I held him, destruction of our old foe was assured:

I savoured that a little. Then I savoured his shielding us from
the spirit that drives France. As you taught me, the spirit is
        inseparable—
thus the honour of two wronged ladies tipped my decision.
Such moments, not I, are the shadow of God upon Earth.—

Aimée Dubucq de Rivéry, mother of the Sultan,
walks in her pavilion, her son's letter trailing in her hand,
and the carpets are a beach far beyond the Barbary pirates.
There she skips with Marie-Josèphe, her poor first cousin,

but *poor* concerns parents only. A black manservant
attends each girl, as they splash filigree in the tide-edge
and gather it, as coral and pierced shells, which the men receive
for in that age young women are free, and men are passive.

Glaze

Tiles are mostly abstract:
tiles come from Islam:
tiles have been through fire:
tiles are a sacred charm:

After the unbearable parallel
trajectories of lit blank tile,
figure-tiles restore the plural,
figuring resumes its true vein.

Harm fades from the spirit as tiles
repeat time beyond time their riddle,
neat stanzas that rhyme from the middle
styles with florets with tendrils of balm.

Henna and mulberry mos-
aics controvert space:
lattice on lattice recedes
through itself into Paradise

or parrot starbursts framing themes
of stars bursting, until they salaam
the Holy Name in sprigged consonants
crosslaced as Welsh metrical schemes.

Conjunct, the infinite doorways
of the mansions of mansions amaze
underfoot in a cool court, with sun-blaze
afloat on the hard water of glaze.

Ur shapes under old liquor
ziggurats of endless incline;
cruciform on maiolica
flourishes the true vine.

Tulip tiles on the grate of Humoresque
Villa join, by a great arabesque,

cream boudoirs of Vienna, then by left–
handed rhyme, the blue pubs of Delft

and prominence stands in a circle
falling to the centre of climb:
O miming is defeated by mime:
circles circle the PR of ominence.

Cool Mesach in fused Rorschach,
old from beyond Islam,
tiles have been to Paradise,
clinkers of ghostly calm.

Shale Country

Watermelon rinds around the house,
small gondolas of curling green
lined with sodden rosy plush;
concrete paths edged with kerosene,

tricycles and shovels in the yard
where the septic tank makes a fairy ring;
a wire gate leads into standing wheat,
cream weatherboard overlaps everything—

and on the wheatless side, storm-blue
plaques curl off the spotted-gum trees
which, in new mayonnaise trunks, stand over
a wheelbarrow on its hands and knees.

▮ The International Terminal

Some comb oil, some blow air,
some shave trenchlines in their hair
but the common joint thump, the heart's spondee
kicks off in its rose-lit inner sea
like an echo, at first, of the one above
it on the dodgy ladder of love—
and my mate who's driving says, *I never
found one yet worth staying with forever.*
In this our poems do not align.
Surely most are if you are, answers mine,
and I am living proof of it,
I gloom, missing you from the cornering outset—
and hearts beat mostly as if they weren't there,
rocking horse to rocking chair,
most audible dubbed on the tracks of movies
or as we approach where our special groove is
or our special fear. The autumn-vast
parking-lot-bitumen overcast
now switches on pumpkin-flower lights
all over dark green garden sites
and a wall of car-bodies, stacked by blokes,
obscures suburban signs and smokes.
Like coughs, cries, all such unlearned effects
the heartbeat has no dialects
but what this or anything may mean
depends on what poem we're living in.
Now a jet engine, huge child of a gun,
shudders with haze and begins to run.
Over Mount Fuji and the North Pole
I'm bound for Europe in a reading role
and a poem long ago that was coming for me
had Fuji-san as its axle-tree.
Cities shower and rattle over the gates
as I enter that limbo between states
but I think of the heart swarmed round by poems

like an egg besieged by chromosomes
and how out of that our world is bred
through the back of a mirror, with clouds in its head
—and airborne, with a bang, this five-hundred-seat
theatre folds up its ponderous feet.

Mirror-glass Skyscrapers

Jade suits pitched frameless up the sky
drift all day with sheer weather,
annexed cubes ascend and blend
at chisel points away high
on talc–green scintillant towers,

diurnal float glass apparitions:
through their aspects airliners flow,
their decoration's anything that happens.
Even their height above suburb
is reflected. Perfect borrowers' rococo!

Outside, squared, has finally gone in,
closed over like steadying water,
to quote storms, to entertain strapped gondolas
and loose giants swimming in contour.
Inside yearning out isn't seen;

work's turned its back on sweat brilliantly—
but when they start to loom, these towers
disappear. Dusk's lightswitches reveal
yellow Business branching kilotall
and haloed with stellar geometry.

Dog Fox Field

The test for feeblemindedness was, they had to make up a
sentence using the words dog, fox *and* field.

Judgement at Nuremberg

These were no leaders, but they were first
into the dark on Dog Fox Field:

Anna who rocked her head, and Paul
who grew big and yet giggled small,

Irma who looked Chinese, and Hans
who knew his world as a fox knows a field.

Hunted with needles, exposed, unfed,
this time in their thousands they bore sad cuts

for having gaped, and shuffled, and failed
to field the lore of prey and hound

they then had to thump and cry in the vans
that ran while stopped in Dog Fox Field.

Our sentries, whose holocaust does not end,
they show us when we cross into Dog Fox Field.

Words of the Glassblowers

In a tacky glass–foundry yard, that is shadowy and bright
as an old painter's sweater stiffening with light,

another lorry chockablock with bottles gets the raised thumb
and there hoists up a wave like flashbulbs feverish in a stadium

before all mass, nosedive and ditch, colour showering to grit,
starrily, mutually, becoming the crush called cullet

which is fired up again, by a thousand degrees, to a mucilage
and brings these reddened spearmen bantering on stage.

Each fishes up a blob, smoke-sallow with a tinge of beer,
which begins, at a breath, to distill from weighty to clear

and, spinning, is inflated to a word: the paraison
to be marvered on iron, box-moulded, or whispered to while
    spun—

Sand, sauce-bottle, hourglass—we melt them into one thing:
that old Egyptian syrup, that tightens as we teach it to sing.

High Sugar

Honey gave sweetness
to Athens and Rome,
and later, when splendour
might rise nearer home,

sweetness was still honey
since, pious or lax,
every cloister had its apiary
for honey and wax

but when kings and new doctrines
drained those deep hives
then millions of people
were shipped from their lives

to grow the high sugar
from which were refined
frigates, perukes, human races
and the liberal mind.

On Removing Spiderweb

Like summer silk its denier
but stickily, oh, ickilier,
miffed bunny-blinder, silver tar,
gesticuli-gesticular,
crepe when cobbed, crap when rubbed,
stretchily adhere-and-there
and everyway, nap-snarled or sleek,
glibly hubbed with grots to tweak:
ehh weakly bobbined tae yer neb,
spit it Phuoc Tuy! filthy web!

The Assimilation of Background

Driving on that wide jute-coloured country
we came at last to the station,
its homestead with lawn and steel awnings
like a fortress against the sun.
And when we knocked, no people answered;
only a black dog came politely
and accompanied us round the verandahs
as we peered into rooms, and called brightly,
Anyone home? The billiard room,
shadowed dining room, gauze-tabled kitchen
gave no answer. Cricket bats, ancient
steamer trunks, the chugging coolroom engine
disregarded us. Only the dog's very patient
claws ticked with us out of the gloom
to the grounds' muffling dust, to the machine shed
black with oil and bolts, with the welder
mantis-like on its cylinder of clocks
and then to the stallion's enclosure.
The great bay horse came up to the wire,
gold flares shifting on his muscles, and stood
as one ungelded in a thousand
of his race, but imprisoned for his sex,
a gene-transmitting engine, looking at us
gravely as a spirit, out between
his brain's potent programmes. Then a heifer,
Durham-roan, but with Brahman hump and rings
around her eyes, came and stood among us
and a dressy goat in sable and brushed fawn
ogled us for offerings beyond
the news all had swiftly gathered from us
in silence, and could, it seemed, accept.
We had been received, and no one grew impatient
but only the dog, host-like, walked with us
back to our car. The lawn-watering sprays
ticked over, and over. And we saw
that out on that bare, crusted country
background and foreground had merged;
nothing that existed there was background.

Accordion Music

A backstrapped family Bible that consoles virtue and sin,
for it opens top and bottom, and harps both out and in:

it shuffles a deep pack of cards, flirts an inverted fan
and stretches to a shelf of books about the pain of man.

It can play the sob in Jesus!, the cavernous *baastards* note,
it can wheedle you for cigarettes or drop a breathy quote:

it can conjure Paris up, or home, unclench a chinstrap jaw
but it never sang for a nob's baton, or lured the boys to war.

Underneath the lone streetlight outside a crossroads hall
where bullocks pass and dead girls waltz and mental gum trees fall

two brothers play their plough-rein days and long gone spoon-
    licked nights.
The fiddle stitching through this quilt lifts up in singing flights,

the other's mourning, meaning tune goes arching up and down
as life undulates like a heavy snake through the rocked accordion.

Slip

This week, one third of Australia is under water.

—Sydney newspaper report, 9 April 1989

Over the terra cotta
speeds a mirrored sun
on bare and bush-mossed water
as a helicopter's stutter
signals a stock-feed run,

and cubic fodder-bombs splash
open on sodden islands.
In their yolk of orange squash,
tugging out each mud galosh,
sheep climb those twenty-inch highlands.

and vehicles at a miles-wide rushing
break in the human map
stare mesmerised at the whooshing
pencil strokes that kink where a crushing
car rolls, and turns on like a tap.

A realised mirage reaches
into tack-sheds and yards
and laps undreamed-of beaches
wadded with shock-tranced creatures.
Millennia of red-walled clouds

have left the creekbeds unable
to let the spreading glaze
spill off the water table,
though here and there a cable
braids light between crumbling cays.

Ariel

Upward, cheeping, on huddling wings,
these small brown mynas have gained
a keener height than their kind ever sustained
but whichever of them fails first
falls to the hawk circling under
who drove them up.
Nothing's free when it is explained.

▍ Politics and Art

Brutal policy,
like inferior art, knows
whose fault it all is.

■ The Ballad of the Barbed-Wire Ocean

No more rice pudding. Pink coupons for Plume. Smokes under
   the lap for aunts.
Four running black boots beside a red sun. Flash wireless words
   like Advawnce.
When the ocean was wrapped in barbed wire, terror radiant up
   the night sky,
exhilaration raced flat out in squadrons; Mum's friends took off
   sun-hats to cry.

Starting south of the then world with new showground rifles
   being screamed at and shown
for a giggle-suit three feeds a day and no more plans of your own,
it went with some swagger till God bless you, Tom! and Daddy
   come back! at the train
or a hoot up the gangways for all the girls and soon the coast
   fading in rain,

but then it was flared screams from blood-bundles whipped rolling
   as iron bombs keened down
and the insect-eyed bombers burned their crews alive in off-
   register henna and brown.
In steep ruins of rainforest pre-affluent thousands ape-scuttling
   mixed sewage with blood
and fear and the poem played vodka to morals, fear jolting to the
   mouth like cud.

It was sleep atop supplies, it was pickhandle, it was coming against
   the wall in tears,
sometimes it was factory banter, stoking jerked breechblocks and
   filing souvenirs,
or miles-wide humming cattleyards of humans, or oiled ship-fires
   slanting in ice,
rag-wearers burst as by huge War Bonds coins, girls' mouths full of
   living rice.

No one came home from it. Phantoms smoked two hundred
   daily. Ghosts held civilians at bay,

since war turns beyond strut and adventure to keeping what
   you've learned, and shown,
what you've approved, and what you've done, from ever reaching
   your own.
This is died for. And nihil and nonsense feed on it day after day.

■ Midnight Lake

Little boy blue, four hours till dawn.
Your bed's a cement bag, your plastic is torn.

Your breakfast was tap water, dinner was sleep;
you are the faith your olds couldn't keep.

In your bunny rug room there were toys on the floor
but nothing is obvious when people get poor

and newspaper crackles next to your skin.
You're a newspaper fairytale now, Tommy Thin,

a postnatal abortion, slick outer space thing,
you run like a pinball BING! smack crack BING!

then, strung out and spotty, you wriggle and sigh
and kiss all the fellows and make them all die.

Antarctica

Beyond the human flat earths
which, policed by warm language, wreathe
in fog the limits of the world,
far out in space you can breathe

the planet revolves in a cold book.
It turns one numb white page a year.
Round this in shattering billions spread
ruins of a Ptolemaic sphere,

and brittle-beard reciters bore
out time in adamant hoar rods
to freight where it's growing short,
childless absolutes shrieking the odds.

Most modern of the Great South Lands,
her storm-blown powder whited wigs
as wit of the New Contempt chilled her.
The first spacefarers worked her rope rigs

in horizontal liftoff, when to climb
the high Pole was officer class.
Total prehuman pavement, extending
beyond every roof-brink of crevasse:

Sterility Park, ringed by sheathed animals.
Singing spiritoso their tongueless keens
musselled carollers fly under the world.
Deeper out, our star's gale folds and greens.

Blue miles above the first flowered hills
towers the true Flood, as it was,
as it is, at the crux of global lattice,
and long-shod humans, risking diamond, steam
propitiating it with known laws and our wickedness.

Blue Roan

for Philip Hodgins

As usual up the Giro mountain
dozers were shifting the road about
but the big blue ranges looked permanent
and the stinging-trees held no hint of drought.

All the high drill and blanket ridges
were dusty for want of winter rains
but down in the creases of picnic oak
brown water moved like handled chains.

Steak-red Herefords, edged like steaks
with that creamy fat the health trade bars,
nudged, feeding, settling who'd get horned
and who'd horn, in the Wingham abattoirs

and men who remembered drought-time grass
like three days' growth on a stark red face
described farms on the creeks, fruit trees and fun
and how they bought out each little place.

Where farm families once would come just to watch
men knock off work, on the Bulliac line,
the fear of helplessness still burned live brush.
Dirty white smoke sent up its scattered sign

and in at the races and out at home
the pump of morale was primed and bled:
"Poor Harry in the street, beer running out his eyes,"
as the cousin who married the baker said.

An Era

The poor were fat and the rich were lean.
Nearly all could preach, very few could sing.
The fashionable were all one age, and to them
a church picnic was the very worst thing.

Wagtail

Willy Wagtail
sings at night
black and white
Oz nightingale
   picks spiders off wall
   nest-fur and eyesocket
   ticks off cows
   cattle love that
Busy daylong
eating small species
makes little faeces
and a great wealth of song
   Will and Willa Wagtail
   indistinguishable
   switchers, whizzers
   drinkers out of scissors
   weave a tiny unit
   kids clemming in it
Piping in tizzes
two fight off one
even one eagle
   little gun swingers
   rivertop ringers
   one-name-for-all
   whose lives flow by heart
   beyond the liver
   into lives of a feather
Wag it here, Willy
pretty it there
flicker and whirr—
if you weren't human
how many would care?

Lyre Bird

Liar made of leaf–litter, quivering ribby in shim,
hen-sized under froufrou, chinks in a quiff display him
or her, dancing in mating time, or out. And in any order.
Tailed mimic aeon-sent to intrigue the next recorder,
I mew catbird, I saw crosscut, I howl she-dingo, I kink
forest hush distinct with bellbirds, warble magpie garble, link
cattlebell with kettle-boil; I rank ducks' cranky presidium
or simulate a triller like a rill mirrored lyrical to a rim.
I ring dim. I alter nothing. Real to real only I sing,
Gahn the crane to Gun the chainsaw, urban thing to being,
Screaming Woman owl and human talk: eedieAi and
    uddyunnunoan.
The miming is all of I. Silent, they are a function
of wet forest, cometary lyrebirds. Their flight lifts them barely a
    semitone.

Shoal

Eye-and-eye eye an eye
each. What blinks is I,
unison of the whole shoal. Thinks:
a dark idea circling by—
again the eyes' I winks.
Eye-and-eye near no eye
is no I, though gill-pulse drinks
and nervy fins spacewalk. Jinx
jets the jettisoned back into all,
tasting, each being a tongue,
vague umbrations of chemical:
this way thrilling, that way Wrong,
the pure always inimical,
compound being even the sheer thing
I suspend I in, and thrust
against, for speed and feeding,
all earblades for the eel's wave-gust
over crayfishes' unpressured beading,
for bird-dive boom, redfin's gaped gong—

Cattle Ancestor

Darrambawli and all his wives, they came feeding from the south-
        east
back in that first time. Darrambawli is a big red fellow,
terrible fierce. He scrapes up dust, singing, whirling his bullroarers
in the air: he swings them and they sing out Crack! Crack!
All the time he's mounting his women, all the time more *kulka*,
more, more, smelling their *kulka* and looking down his nose.
Kangaroo and emu mobs run from him, as he tears up their
        shelters,
throwing the people in the air, stamping out their fires.
Darrambawli gathers up his brothers, all making that sad cry *mar
        mar*:
he initiates his brothers, the Bulluktruk. They walk head down in
        a line
and make the big blue ranges. You hear their clinking noise in
        there.
Darrambawli has wives everywhere, he has to gallop back and
        forth,
mad for their *kulka*. You see him on the coast, and on the plains.
They're eating up the country, so the animals come to spear them:
You have to die now, you're starving us. But then Waark the crow
tells Darrambawli, Your wives, they're spearing them. He is
        screaming,
frothing at the mouth, that's why his chest is all white nowadays.
Jerking two knives, he screams, *I make new waterholes! I bring the
        best song!*
He makes war on all that mob, raging, dotting the whole country.
He frightens the water-snakes; they run away, they can't sit down.
The animals forget how to speak. There is only one song
for a while. Darrambawli must sing it on his own.

■ Mollusc

By its nobship sailing upside down,
by its inner sexes, by the crystalline
pimplings of its skirts, by the sucked-on
lifelong kiss of its toppling motion,
by the viscose optics now extruded
now wizened instantaneously, by the
ridges grating up a food-path, by
the pop shell in its nick of dry,
by excretion, the earthworm coils, the glibbing,
by the gilt slipway, and by pointing
perhaps as far back into time as
ahead, a shore being folded interior,
by boiling on salt, by coming uncut over
a razor's edge, by hiding the Oligocene
underleaf may this and every snail sense
itself ornament the weave of presence.

Echidna

Crumpled in a coign I was milk-tufted with my suckling
till he prickled.
He entered the earth pouch then
and learned ant-ribbon,
the gloss we put like lightning on the brimming ones.
Life is fat is sleep. I feast life on and sleep it,
deep loveself in calm.
I awaken to spikes of food-sheathing, of mulling fertile egg,
of sun, of formic gravels,
of worms, dab hunting, of fanning under quill-ruff when budged:
all are rinds, to sleep.
Corner-footed tongue-scabbard, I am trundling doze
and wherever I put it
is exactly right. Sleep goes there.

Shellback Tick

Match-head   of groins
nailhead   in fur
blank   itch   of blank
the blood   thereof
is the strength thereof is
the jellied life-breath   is O the
sweet incision   so the curdy reed
floodeth sun-hot liquor the only ichor the only
thing which existeth wholly alley-echoing
duple rhythmic feed which same of great yore turned
my back on every other thing the mothering thereof
the seed whereof in need-clotting strings
of plaque I dissolve with reagent drool
that doth stagger swelling's occult throb.
O one tap of splendour turned to me—
blank years   grass grip
sun   haggard   rain
shell to that all.

Cell DNA

I am the singular
in free fall.
I and my doubles
carry it all:

life's slim volume
spirally bound.
It's what I'm about,
it's what I'm around.

Presence and hungers
imbue a sap mote
with the world as they spin it.
I teach it by rote

but its every command
was once a miscue
that something rose to,
Presence and freedom

re-wording, re-beading
strains on a strand
making I and I more different
than we could stand.

Goose to Donkey

My big friend, I bow help;
I bow, Get up, big friend:
let me land-swim again beside your clicky feet,
don't sleep flat with dried wet in your holes.

Spermaceti

I sound my sight, and flexing skeletons eddy
in our common wall. With a sonic bolt from the fragrant
chamber of my head, I burst the lives of some
and slow, backwashing them into my mouth. I lighten,
breathe, and laze below again. And peer in long low tones
over the curve of Hard to river-tasting and oil-tasting
coasts, to the grand grinding coasts of rigid air.
How the wall of our medium has a shining, pumping rim:
the withstood crush of deep flight in it, perpetual entry!
Only the holes of eyesight and breath still tie us
to the dwarf-making Air, where true sight barely functions.
The power of our wall likewise guards us from
slowness of the rock Hard, its life-powdering compaction,
from its fissures and streamy layers that we sing into sight
but are silent, fixed, disjointed in. Eyesight is a leakage
of nearby into us, and shows us the tastes of food
conformed over its spines. But our greater sight is uttered.
I sing beyond the curve of distance the living joined bones
of my song-fellows; I sound a deep volcano's valve tubes
storming whitely in black weight; I receive an island's slump,
song-scrambling ship's heartbeats, and the sheer shear of current-
    forms
bracketing a seamount. The wall, which running blind I demolish,
heals, prickling me with sonars. My every long shaped cry
re-establishes the world, and centres its ringing structure.

Migratory

I am the nest that comes and goes,
I am the egg that isn't now,
I am the beach, the food in sand,
the shade with shells and the shade with sticks.
I am the right feeling on washed shine,
in wing-lifting surf, in running about
beak-focused: the feeling of here, that stays
and stays, then lengthens out over
the hill of hills and the feedy sea.
I am the wrongness of here, when it
is true to fly along the feeling
the length of its great rightness, while days
burn from vast to a gold gill in the dark
to vast again, for many feeds
and floating rests, till the sun ahead
becomes the sun behind, and half
the little far days of the night are different.
Right feelings of here arrive with me:
I am the nests danced for and now,
I am the crying heads to fill,
I am the beach, the sand in food,
the shade with sticks and the double kelp shade.

The Fellow Human

Beside Anchor Flour school frocks dimmed with redknuckle soaps
poverty's hardly poverty nowadays, here.
The mothers who drive up under tortoiseshell pines to the school
are neat in jeans and track tops
and have more self and presence on hand in the car.

Their four-wheeled domains are compound of doors to slam
but only their children do. Drama is private, for home.
Here, the tone is citizenly equal.
The woman with timber-grey braids and two modelled in cold-
     cream
chat through and minutely modulate their opening wry smile.

Another, serene, makes a sad-comic mouth beneath glasses
for her fine-necked rugby-mad boy, also in glasses,
and registers reed notes in the leatherhead birds' knotty music
as they unpick a red-gold judge's wig of bloom
in the silky-oak tree above the school's two classes.

To remodel the countryside, in this post-job age of peace,
they have slept with trucks, raised houses by hammer and
     telephone,
plucked sopping geese and whitened them to stone,
and suddenly most sex writing seems slave-era boasting, in the
     face,
living mousseline, never-shaved, of the fellow human.

The ginger local woman alighting from the saddle of her van
talks to a new friend who balances a baby on one hip
and herself on the other. The two nod upwards, and laugh.
Not for heavy old reasons does the one new here go barefoot
but to be arrived, at home in this dust-warm landscape.

▌ The Wedding at Berrico

Christina and James, 8 February 1992

To reach your watershed country
we've driven this summer's green climbs
and the creekwater film spooling over
causeways got spliced many times
with its boulders like ice under whisky,
tree pools mirrory as the eyes of horses.
Great hills above, the house *en fête*:
we've parked between soaring rhymes
and slipped in among brilliant company.

Here are your gifts. I see God's sent
all your encounters so far with him:
life. Landscape. Unfraught love. Some poetry.
Risk too, with his star rigger Freedom,
but here's poise, for whatever may come.
What's life wish you? Sound genetics, delight,
long resilience against gravity, the sight
of great-grandchildren, a joint sense of home.

Hey, all these wishes in smart boxes! Fun,
challenges, Meaning, work-satisfaction—
this must be the secular human lot: health
till high old age, children of character,
dear friendships. And the testing one: wealth.
Quietly we add ours: may you
always have each other, and want to.

Few poems I've made mention our children.
That I write at all got you dork names.
More might have brought worse. Our jealous nation . . .
I am awed at you, though, today,
silk restraining your briskness and gumption,
my mother's face still hauntingly in yours

and this increase, this vulnerable beauty.

James is worthy of his welcome to our family.
Never would I do, or he ask
me to do what no parental memories
could either: I won't give you away.

But now you join hands, exchanging
the vows that cost joyfully dear.
They move you to the centre of life
and us gently to the rear.

The Say-but-the-Word Centurion
Attempts a Summary

That numinous healer who preached Saturnalia and paradox
    has died a slave's death. We were manoeuvred into it by priests
and by the man himself. To complete his poem.

He was certainly dead. The pilum guaranteed it. His message,
unwritten except on his body, like anyone's, was wrapped
like a scroll and despatched to our liberated selves, the gods.

If he has now risen, as our infiltrators gibber,
he has outdone Orpheus, who went alive to the Shades.
Solitude may be stronger than embraces. Inventor of the mustard
    tree,

he mourned one death, perhaps all, before he reversed it.
He forgave the sick to health, disregarded the sex of the Furies
when expelling them from minds. And he never speculated.

If he is risen, all are children of a most high real God
or something even stranger called by that name
who knew to come and be punished for the world.

To have knowledge of right, after that, is to be in the wrong.
Death came through the sight of law. His people's oldest wisdom.
If death is now the birth-gate into things unsayable

in language of death's era, there will be wars about religion
as there never were about the death-ignoring Olympians.
Love, too, his new universal, so far ahead of you it has died

for you before you meet it, may seem colder than the favours of
    gods
who are our poems, good and bad. But there never was a bad
    baby.
Half of his worship will be grinding his face in the dirt

then lifting it to beg, in private. The low will rule, and curse by
    him.
Divine bastard, soul-usurer, eros-frightener, he is out to
    monopolise hatred.
Whole philosophies will be devised for their brief snubbings of
    him.

But regained excels kept, he taught. Thus he has done the
    impossible
to show us it is there. To ask it of us. It seems we are to be the
    poem
and live the impossible. As each time we have, with mixed cries.

Dead Trees in the Dam

Castle scaffolding tall in moat,
the dead trees in the dam
flower each morning with birds.

It can be just the three resident
cormorants with musket-hammer necks, plus
the clinician spoonbill, its long pout;

twilight's herons who were almost too lightfoot
to land; pearl galahs in pink-fronted
confederacy, each starring in its frame.

or it may be a misty candelabrum
of egrets lambent before Saint Sleep—
who gutter awake and balance stiffly off.

Odd mornings, it's been all bloodflag
and rifle green: a stopped-motion shrapnel
of kingparrots. Smithereens when they freaked.

Rarely, it's wed ducks, whose children
will float among the pillars. In daytime
magpies sidestep up wood to jag pinnacles

and the big blow-in cuckoo crying
Alarm, Alarm on the wing is not let light.
This hours after dynastic charts of high

profile ibis have rowed away to beat
the paddocks. Which, however green, are
always watercolour, and on brown paper.

The Rollover

Some of us primary producers, us farmers and authors,
are going round to watch them evict a banker.
It'll be sad. I hate it when the toddlers and wives
are out beside the fence, crying, and the big kids
wear that thousand-yard stare common in all refugees.
Seeing home desecrated as you lose it can do that to you.

There's the ute piled high with clothes and old debentures.
There's the faithful VDU, shot dead, still on its lead.
This fellow's dad and grandad were bankers before him, they
    sweated
through the old hard inspections, had years of brimming
    foreclosure,
but here it all ends. He'd lent three quarters and only
asked for a short extension. Six months. But you have to

line the drawer somewhere. You have to be kind to be cruel.
It's Sydney or the cash these times. Who buys the Legend of the
    Bank
anymore? The laconic teller, the salt-of-the-earth branch
    accountant,
it's all an Owned Boys story. Now they reckon he's grabbed a gun
and an old coin sieve and holed up in the vault, screaming
about his years of work, his identity. Queer talk from a bank-
    johnny!

We're catching flak, too, from a small mob of his mates,
inbred under-manager types, here to back him up. Troublemakers,
land-despoiling white trash. It'll do them no good. Their turn
is coming. They'll be rationalised themselves, made adapt
to a multinational society. There's no room in that for privileged
traditional ways of life. No land rights for bankers.

Corniche

I work all day and hardly drink at all.
I can reach down and feel if I'm depressed.
I adore the Creator because I made myself
and a few times a week a wire jags in my chest.

The first time, I'd been coming apart all year.
weeping, incoherent; cigars had given me up:
any road round a cliff edge I'd whimper along in low gear
then: cardiac horror. Masking my pulse's calm lub-dub.

It was the victim-sickness. Adrenaline howling in my head,
the black dog was my brain. Come to drown me in my breath
was energy's black hole, depression, compere of the predawn show
when, returned from a pee, you stew and welter in your death.

The rogue space rock is on course to snuff your world,
sure. But go acute, and its oncoming fills your day.
The brave die but once? I could go a hundred times a week,
clinging to my pulse with the world's edge inches away.

Laugh, who never shrank around wizened genitals there
or killed themselves to stop dying. The blow that never falls
batters you stupid. Only gradually do
you notice a slight scorn in you for what appals.

A self inside self, cool as conscience, one to be erased
in your final night, or faxed, still knows beneath
all the mute grand opera and uncaused effect—
that death which can be imagined is not true death.

▋ Suspended Vessels

for Joanna Gooding and Simon Curtis

Here is too narrow and brief:
equality and justice, to be real,
require the timeless. It argues
afterlife even to name them.

I've thought this more since that morning
in barren country vast as space-time
but affluent with cars
at the fence where my tightening budget
denied me basket-room
under the haunches of a hot-air balloon

and left thirteen people in it,
all ages, teens to grans,
laughing excitedly as the dragon nozzle
exhaled hoarse blazing lift, tautening it,
till they grabbed, dragged, swayed
up, up into their hiatus.

Others were already aloft,
I remember, light bulbs against the grizzled
mountain ridge and bare sky,
vertical yachts, with globe spinnakers.

More were being rigged, or offering
their gape for gusts of torch.
I must have looked away—
suddenly a cry erupted everywhere:
two, far up, lay overlapping,
corded and cheeked as the foresails of a ship
but tangled, and one collapsing.

I suppress in my mind
the long rag unravelling, the mixed
high voice of its spinning fall,

the dust-blast crash, the privacies
and hideous equality without justice
of those thirteen, which running helpers,
halting, must have seen
and professionals lifted out.

Instead, I look at coloured cash and plastic
and toddlerhood's vehement equities
that are never quite silenced.
Indeed, it prickles, and soon glares
if people do not voice them.

■ The Water Column

We had followed the catwalk upriver
by flowering trees and granite sheer
to the Basin park crying with peacocks.

After those, we struck human conversation.
A couple we'd thought Austrian proved to be
Cape Coloured. Wry good sense and lore

and love of their strange country
they presented us with, cheerfully.
They were eager "to get home for the riots."

As we talked, shoes dreamily, continually
passed above us on the horizontal chairlift.
It was Blundstones and joggers that year,

cogwheel treads with faces between them.
That was also the year I learned
the Basin was a cold crater lake:

swimmers whacking above ancient drownings—
"It's never been plumbed, in places."
I thought of a rock tube of water

down, down levels too frigid for upwelling,
standing at last on this miles-deep
lager head, above a live steam layer

in impossible balance, facing
where there can't be water, the planet's
convecting inner abortive iron star.

The Beneficiaries

Higamus hogamus
Western intellectuals
never praise Auschwitz.
Most ungenerous. Most odd,
when they claim it's what finally
won them their centuries-
long war against God.

Like Wheeling Stacked Water

Dried nests in the overhanging limbs
are where the flood hatched eggs of swirl.
Like is unscary milder love. More can be in it.

The flood boomed up nearly to the door
like a taxiing airliner. It flew past all day.
Now the creek is down to barley colour
waist deep on her, chest on him,
wearing glasses all around them, barely pushing.

Down under stops of deadwood pipe in living
branches, they move on again. The bottom
is the sunk sand cattle-road they know
but hidden down cool, and mincing
magically away at every step, still going.

The wide creek is a tree hall decorated
with drowned and tobacco ribbons,
with zippy tilting birds, with dried snakes hanging
over the doorways everywhere along.

They push on. *Say this log I'm walking*
under the water's a mast like off a
olden day ship— Fine hessian shade
is moistening down off cross-trees,

and like wings, the rocking waterline
gloving up and down their bodies
pumps support to their swimmy planet steps.

They've got a hook and bits
of bluebottle line from salt holidays.
They had a poor worm, and crickets automatic in a jar,
but they let all them off fishing.

They're taking like to an adventure instead,
up past there where the undercut bank

makes that bottling noise, and the kingfisher's
beak is like the weight he's thrown by
to fly him straight.

By here, they're wheeling stacked-up water.
It has mounted like mild ice bedclothes to
their chest and chin. They have to tiptoe
under all the white davits of the bush.

But coming to the island that is like the pupil
in acres of eye, their clothes pour water
off like heavy chain. They toil, and lighten
as they go up on it. All this is like the past
but none of it is sad. It has never ended.

Wallis Lake Estuary

(from "The Sand Coast Sonnets")

for Valerie

A long street of all blue windows,
the estuary bridge is double-humped
like a bullock yoke. The north tide
teems through to four arriving rivers,
the south tide works the sinus channel
to the big heart-shaped real estate lake.
Both flood oyster farms like burnt floor joists
that islands sleep out among like dogs.

Glorious on a brass day the boiling up
from the south, of a storm above those paddocks
of shoal-creamed, wake-dolphined water.
Equally at dusk, when lamps and pelicans
are posted, the persistence of dark lands
out there on the anodised light void.

Memories of the Height-to-Weight Ratio

I was a translator in the Institute back
when being accredited as a poet
meant signing things against Vietnam.
For scorn of the bargain I wouldn't do it.

And the Institute was after me
to lose seven teeth and five stone in weight
and pass their medical. Three years I dodged
then offered the teeth under sacking threat.

From five to nine, in warm Lane Cove,
and five to nine again at night,
an irascible Carpatho-Ruthenian strove
with ethnic teeth. He claimed the bite

of a human determined their intelligence.
More gnash-power sent the brain more blood.
In Hungarian, Yiddish or Serbo-Croat
he lectured emotional fur-trimmers good,

clacking a jointed skull in his hand,
and sent them to work face-numbed and bright.
This was my wife's family dentist. He
looked into my mouth, blenched at the sight,

eclipsed me with his theory of occlusion,
and wrested and tugged. Pausing to blow
out cigarette smoke, he'd bite his only
accent-free mother tongue and return below

to raise my black fleet of sugar-barques
so anchored that they gave him tennis elbow.
Seven teeth I gave that our babies might eat
when students were chanting Make Love! Hey Ho!

But there was a line called Height-to-Weight
and a parallel line on Vietnam. When a tutor

in politics failed all who crossed that, and wasn't
dismissed, scholarship was back to holy writ.

Fourteen pounds were a stone, and of great yore so,
but the doctor I saw next had no schoolyard in him:
You're a natural weight-lifter! Come join my gym!
Sonnets of flesh could still model my torso.

Modernism's not modern: it's police and despair.
I wear it as fat, and it gnawed off my hair
as my typewriter clicked over gulfs and birch spaces
where the passive voice muffled enormity and faces.

But when the Institute started afresh
to circle my job, we decamped to Europe
and spent our last sixpence on a pig's head.
Any job is a comedown, where I was bred.

On Home Beaches

Back, in my fifties, fatter than I was then,
I step on the sand, belch down slight horror to walk
a wincing pit edge, waiting for the pistol-shot
laughter. Long greening waves cash themselves, foam change
sliding into Ocean's pocket. She turns: ridicule looks down,
strappy, with faces averted, or is glare and families.
The great hawk of the beach is outstretched, point to point,
quivering and hunting. Cars are the surf at its back.
You peer, at this age, but it's still there, ridicule,
the pistol that kills women, that gets them killed, crippling
    men
on the towel-spattered sand. Equality is dressed, neatly,
with mouth still shut. Bared body is not equal ever.
Some are smiled to each other. Many surf, swim, play ball:
like that red boy, holding his wet T-shirt off his breasts.

Water-Gardening in an Old Farm Dam

Blueing the blackened water
that I'm widening with my spade
as I lever up water tussocks
and chuck them ashore like sopping comets
is a sun-point, dazzling heatless
acetylene, under tadpoles that swarm
wobbling, like a species of flies
and buzzing bubbles that speed
upward like many winged species.

Unwettable green tacos are lotus leaves.
Waterlily leaves are notched plaques
of the water. Their tubers resemble
charred monstera trunks. Some I planted.
some I let float. And I bought
thumb-sized mosquito-eating fish
for a dollar in a plastic amnion.
"Wilderness" says we've lost belief
in human building: our dominance
now so complete that we hide from it.

Where, with my levered back,
I stand, too late in life,
in a populous amber, feet deep
in digesting chyle over clays,
I love green humanised water
in old brick pounds, water carried
unleaking for miles around contour,
or built out into, or overstepping
stonework in long frilled excess.

The hands' pride and abysmal
pay that such labour earned,
as against the necks and billions
paid for Nature. But the workers
and the need are gone, without reaching
here: this was never canal country.

It's cow-ceramic, softened at rain times,
where the kookaburra's laugh
is like angles of a scrubbing toothbrush
heard through the bones of the head.

Level water should turn out of sight,
on round a bend, behind an island,
in windings of possibility, not
be exhausted in one gesture, like an avenue.
It shouldn't be surveyable in one look.
That's a waterhole. Still, the trees
I planted along this one bend it
a bit, and half roof it, bringing
its wet underearth shadow to the surface
as shade. And the reeds I hate,

mint sheaves, human-high palisades
that would close in round the water,
I could fire floating petrol among them
again, and savage but not beat them,
or I could declare them beautiful.

It Allows a Portrait in Line-Scan at Fifteen

He retains a slight "Martian" accent, from the years of single
phrases,
He no longer hugs to disarm. It is gradually allowing him
affection.
It does not allow proportion. Distress is absolute, shrieking, and
runs him at frantic speed through crashing doors.
He likes cyborgs. Their taciturn power, with his intonation.
It still runs him around the house, alone in the dark, cooing and
laughing.
He can read about soils, populations, and New Zealand. On
neutral topics he's illiterate.
Arnie Schwarzenegger is an actor. He isn't a cyborg really, is he, Dad?
He lives on forty acres, with animals and trees, and used to draw it
continually.
He knows the map of Earth's fertile soils, and can draw it
freehand.
He can only lie in a panicked shout *SorrySorryIdidn'tdoit!* warding
off conflict with others and himself.
When he ran away constantly it was to the greengrocers to
worship stacked fruit.
His favourite country was the Ukraine: it is nearly all deep fertile
soil.
Giggling, he climbed all over the dim Freudian psychiatrist who
told us how autism resulted from "refrigerator" parents.
When asked to smile, he photographs a rictus-smile on his face.
It long forbade all naturalistic films. They were Adult movies.
If they (that is, he) *are bad the police will put them in hospital.*
He sometimes drew the farm amid Chinese or Balinese rice
terraces.
When a runaway, he made uproar in the police station, playing at
three times adults speed.
Only animated films were proper. *Who Framed Roger Rabbit* then
authorised the rest.
Phrases spoken to him he would take as teaching, and repeat.
When he worshipped fruit, he screamed as if poisoned when it
was fed to him.
A one-word first conversation: *Blane—Yes! Plane, that's right,
baby!—Blane.*

He has forgotten nothing, and remembers the precise quality of experiences.

It requires rulings: *Is stealing very playing up, as bad as murder?*

He counts at a glance, not looking. And he has never been lost.

When he ate only nuts and dried fruit, words were for dire emergencies.

He knows all the breeds of fowls, and the counties of Ireland.

He'd begun to talk, then returned to babble, then silence. It withdrew speech for years.

Is that very autistic, to play video games in the day?

He is anger's mirror, and magnifies any near him, raging it down.

It still won't allow him fresh fruit, or orange juice with bits in it.

He swam in the midwinter dam at night. It had no rules about cold.

He was terrified of thunder and finally cried as if in explanation, *It—angry!*

He grilled an egg he'd broken into bread. Exchanges of soil-knowledge are called landtalking.

He lives in objectivity. I was sure Bell's palsy would leave my face only when he said it had begun to.

Don't say word! when he was eight forbade the word "autistic" in his presence.

Bantering questions about girlfriends cause a terrified look and blocked ears.

He sometimes centred the farm in a furrowed American Midwest.

Eye contact, Mum! means he truly wants attention. It dislikes I contact.

He is equitable and kind, and only ever a little jealous. It was a relief when that little arrived.

He surfs, bowls, walks for miles. For many years he hasn't trailed his left arm while running.

I gotta get smart! looking terrified into the years. *I gotta get smart!*

Performance

I starred last night, I shone:
I was footwork and firework in one,

a rocket that wriggled up and shot
darkness with a parasol of brilliants
and a peewee descant on a flung bit;
I was busters of glitter-bombs expanding
to mantle and aurora from a crown,
I was fouettés, falls of blazing paint,
para-flares spot-welding cloudy heaven,
loose gold off fierce toeholds of white,
a finale red-tongued as a haka leap:
that too was a butt of all right!

As usual after any triumph, I was
of course inconsolable.

Australian Love Poem

for Jennifer Strauss

A primary teacher taking courses,
he loved the little girls,
never hard enough to be sacked:
parents made him change schools.

When sure this was his life sentence,
he dropped studies for routine:
the job, the Turf papers, beer,
the then-new poker machine.

Always urbane, he boarded happily
among show-jump ribbons, nailed towels,
stockwhip attitudes he'd find reasons for
and a paddock view, with fowls.

Because the old days weren't connected
the boss wouldn't have the phone.
The wife loved cards, outings, "Danny Boy,"
sweet malice in a mourning tone.

Life had set his hosts aside, as a couple,
from verve or parenthood.
How they lived as a threesome enlivened them
and need not be understood.

Euchre hands that brushed away the decades
also fanned rumour
and mothers of daughters banned the teacher
in his raceday humour,

but snap brim feigning awe of fat-cattle brim
and the henna rinse between them
enlarged each of the three to the others, till
the boss fell on his farm.

Alone together then, beyond the talk,
he'd cook, and tint, and curl,
and sit voluble through rare family visits
to his aged little girl.

As she got lost in the years
where she would wander,
her boy would hold her in bed
and wash sheets to spread under.

But when her relations carried her,
murmuring, out to their van,
he fled that day, as one with no rights,
as an unthanked old man.

Inside Ayers Rock

Inside Ayers Rock is lit
with paired fluorescent lights
on steel pillars supporting the ceiling
of haze-blue marquee cloth
high above the non-slip pavers.
Curving around the cafeteria
throughout vast inner space
is a Milky Way of plastic chairs
in foursomes around tables
all the way to the truck drivers' enclave.
Dusted coolabah trees grow to the ceiling,
TVs talk in gassy colours, and
round the walls are Outback shop fronts:
the Beehive Bookshop for brochures,
Casual Clobber, the bottled Country Kitchen
and the sheet-iron Dreamtime Experience
that is turned off at night.
A high bank of medal-ribbony
lolly jars presides over
island counters like opened crates.
one labelled White Mugs, and covered with them.
A two-dimensional policeman
discourages shoplifting of gifts
and near the entrance, where you pay
for fuel, there stands a tribal man
in rib-paint and pubic tassel.
It is all gentle and kind.
In beyond the children's playworld
there are fossils, like crumpled
old drawings of creatures in rock.

Contested Landscape at Forsayth

The conquest of fire-culture
on that timber countryside
has broadcast innumerable
termite mounds all through
the gravel gold-rush hills
and the remnant railhead town,
petrified French mustards
out of jars long smashed.

Train platform and tin Shire
are beleaguered in nameless cemetery.
Outworks of the Dividing range
are annulled under Dreaming-turds.
It's as if every place a miner
cursed, or thought of sex,
had its abraded marker. Mile
on mile of freckled shade,
the ordinary is riddled by
cylinder-pins of unheard music.

On depopulated country
frail billions are alive
in layered earthen lace.
Their every flight is
a generation, glueing towers
which scatter and mass
on a blind smell-plan.
Cobras and meta-cobras
in the bush, immense black vines
await monsoon in a world
of clay lingam altars.

Like the monuments to every
mortal thing that a planet without God
would require, and inscriptionless
as rage would soon weather those,
the anthills erupt on verges,

on streets, round the glaring pub,
its mango tree and sleeping-fridges,
an estuary of undergrounds,
dried cities of the flying worm.

The Shield-Scales of Heraldry

Surmounting my government's high evasions
stands a barbecue of crosses and birds
tended by a kangaroo and emu,
but in our courts, above the judge,
a lion and a unicorn still keep
their smaller offspring, plus a harp,
in an open prison looped with mottoes.

Coats of arms, plaster Rorschach blots,
crowned stone moths, they encrust Europe.
As God was dismissed from churches
they fluttered in and cling to the walls,
abstract comic-pages held by scrolled beasts,
or wear on the flagstones underfoot.
They pertain to an earlier Antichrist,

the one before police. Mafiose citadels
made them, states of one attended family
islanded in furrows. The oldest
are the simplest. A cross, some coins,
a stripe, a roof tree, a spur rowel,
bowstaves, a hollow-gutted lion,
and all in lucid target colours.

Under tinned heads with reveries tied on,
shields are quartered and cubed by marriage
till they are sacred campaign maps
or anatomy inside dissected mantling,
glyphs minutely clear through their one
rule, that colour must abut either
gold or silver, the non-weapon metals.

The New World doesn't blazon well—
the New World ran away from blazonry
or was sent away in chains by it—
but exceptions shine: the spread eagle
with the fireworks display on its belly

and in the thinks-balloon above its head.
And when as a half-autistic

kid in scrub paddocks vert and or
I grooved on the cloisons of pedigree
it was a vivid writing of system
that hypnotised me, beyond the obvious
euphemism of force. It was eight hundred
years of cubist art and Europe's dreamings:
the Cup, the Rose, the Ship, the Antlers.

High courage, bestial snobbery,
neither now merits ungrace from us.
They could no longer hang me,
throttling, for a rabbit sejant.
Like everyone, I would now be lord
or lady myself, and pardon me
or myself loose the coronet-necked hounds.

Now we face new people who share
attitudes only with each other,
withholding all fellowship with us,
and genial laughter. Reverse nobles
who twist us into Gorgon shapes
of an anti-heraldry, inside
their journals and never-lowered shields.

The Year of the Kiln Portraits

I came in from planting more trees.
I was sweating, and flopped down aslant
on the sofa. You and Clare were sitting
at the lunch table, singing as you do
in harmony even I hear as beautiful,
mezzo-soprano and soprano,
for anything Arno. You winked at me
and, liquescent as my face was,
I must have looked like the year
you painted all our portraits, lovingly,
exquisitely, on ceramic tiles
in undrying oil, just one
or at most two colours at a time,
and carried them braced oblique, wet,
in plastic ice-cream boxes to town.
It was encaustic painting,
ancient Rome's photography, that gets
developed in successive kiln firings
till it lives, time-freed, transposed
in behind a once-blank glaze.
Afterwards, you did some figured tiles
for our patchwork chimney, then stopped.
In art, you have serious gifts. But it's
crazy: you're not driven. Not obsessive.

Tympan Alley

Adult songs in English,
avoiding schmaltz,
pre–twang:
the last songs adults sang.

When roles and manners wore
their cuffs as shot as Or-
tega y Gasset's,
soloists sang

as if a jeweller raised
pinches of facets
for hearts as yet unfazed
by fatty assets.

Adult songs with English;
the brilliantine long-play
records of the day
sing of the singlish,

the arch from wry to rue,
of marques and just one Engel,
blue, that Dietrich played;
euphemism's last parade

with rhymes still on our side
unwilling to divide
the men from the poise,
of lackadays and lakatois—

and always you,
cool independent You.
unsnowable, au fait,
when Us were hotly two,

not lost in They.

A Lego of Driving to Sydney

Dousing the campfire with tea
you step on the pedal and mount
whip-high behind splashboard and socket.
Your burnished rims tilt and rebound
among bristling botany. Only
a day now to the Port,
to bodices in the coffee palace,
to metal-shying razors in suits
and bare ships towing out, to dress
and concentrate in the wind.

  Motoring down the main roads,
  fenced wheeltrack-choices in forest,
  odd scored beds of gravel,
  knotwood in the ground—
  you will have to wrestle
  hand and foot to reach Sydney
  and win every fall.
  River punts are respites.
  Croak-oak! the horsedung roads
  aren't scented any more, but tasted.
  Paved road starts at Chatswood:
  just one ferry then, to stringing
  tramears and curl the mo,
  to palms in the wonderful hotels.

Blazing down a razorback
in slab dark, in a huge
American car of the chassis age
to rescue for pleated cushions
a staring loved one who'll sway
down every totter of the gangway
on cane legs. Petrol coupons
had to be scrounged for this one:
they have seen too much railway.

Queuing down bloody highways
all round Easter, crawling in
to the great herbed sandstone bowl
of tealeaf scrub and suburbs,
hills by Monier and Wunderlich
in kiln orange, with cracks of harbour,
coming down to miss the milking
on full board, with baked Sundays,
life now to be neat and dry eyed,
coming down to be gentrified.

One long glide down the freeway
through aromatic radar zones,
soaring Egyptian rock cuttings
bang into a newsprint-coloured
rainstorm, tweeting the car phone
about union shares and police futures.
Driving in in your thousands
to the Show, to be detained
half a lifetime, or to grow rental
under steel flagpoles lapping
with multicoloured recipes.

Burning Want

From just on puberty, I lived in funeral:
mother dead of miscarriage, father trying to be dead,
we'd boil sweat-brown cloth; cows repossessed the garden.
Lovemaking brought death, was the unuttered principle.

I met a tall adopted girl some kids thought aloof,
but she was intelligent. Her poise of white-blond hair
proved her no kin to the squat tanned couple who loved her.
Only now do I realise she was my first love.

But all my names were fat-names, at my new town school.
Between classes, kids did erocide: destruction of sexual morale.
Mass refusal of unasked love: that works. Boys cheered as
    seventeen-
year-old girls came on to me, then ran back whinnying ridicule.

The slender girl came up on holidays from the city
to my cousins' farm. She was friendly and sane.
Whispers giggled round us. A letter was written as from me
and she was there, in mid-term, instantly.

But I called people "the humans" not knowing it was rage.
I learned things sidelong, taking my rifle for walks,
recited every scene of *From Here to Eternity*, burned paddocks
and soldiered back each Monday to that dawning Teen age.

She I admired, and almost relaxed from placating,
was gnawed by knowing what she came from, not who.
Showing off was my one social skill, oddly never with her,
but I dissembled feelings, till mine were unknown to me too

and I couldn't add my want to her shortfall of wantedness.
I had forty more years, with one dear remission,
of a white paralysis: she's attracted it's not real nothing is enough
she's mistaken she'll die go now! she'll tell any minute she'll
    laugh—

Whether other hands reached out to Marion, or didn't,
at nineteen in her training ward she had a fatal accident
alone, at night, they said, with a lethal injection
and was spared from seeing what my school did to the world.

The Last Hellos

Don't die, Dad—
but they die.

This last year he was wandery:
took off a new chainsaw blade
and cobbled a spare from bits.
Perhaps if I lay down
my head'll come better again.
His left shoulder kept rising
higher in his cardigan.

He could see death in a face.
Family used to call him in
to look at sick ones and say.
At his own time, he was told.

The knob found in his head
was duck-egg size. Never hurt.
Two to six months, Cecil.

I'll be right, he boomed
to his poor sister on the phone.
I'll do that when I finish dyin.

Don't die, Cecil.
But they do.

Going for last drives
in the bush, odd massive

board-slotted stumps bony white
in whipstick second growth.
I could chop all day.

I could always cash
a cheque, in Sydney or anywhere.
Any of the shops.

Eating, still at the head
of the table, he now missed
food on his knife side.

Sorry, Dad, but like
have you forgiven your enemies?
Your father and all them?
All his lifetime of hurt.

I must have (grin). *I don't*
think about that now.

People can't say goodbye
any more. They say last hellos.

Going fast, over Christmas,
he'd still stumble out
of his room, where his photos
hang over the other furniture,
and play host to his mourners.

The courage of his bluster,
firm big voice of his confusion.

Two last days in the hospital:
his long forearms were still
red mahogany. His hands
gripped steel frame. *I'm dyin.*

On the second day:
You're bustin to talk
but I'm too busy dyin.

Grief ended when he died,
the widower like soldiers who
won't live life their mates missed.

Good boy, Cecil! No more Bluey dog.
No more cowtime. No more stories.
We're still using your imagination,
it was stronger than all ours.

Your grave's got littler
somehow, in the three months.
More pointy as the clay's shrivelled,
like a stuck zip in a coat.

Your cricket boots are in
the State museum! Odd letters
still come. Two more's died since you:
Annie, and Stewart. Old Stewart.

On your day there was a good crowd,
family, and people from away.
But of course a lot had gone
to their own funerals first.

Snobs mind us off religion
nowadays, if they can.
Fuck them. I wish you God.

Comete

Uphill in Melbourne on a beautiful day
a woman was walking ahead of her hair.
Like teak oiled soft to fracture and sway
it hung to her heels and seconded her
as a pencilled retinue, an unscrolling title
to ploughland, edged with ripe rows of dress,
a sheathed wing that couldn't fly her at all,
only itself, loosely, and her spirits.
                                    A largesse
of life and self, brushed all calm and out,
its abstracted attempts on her mouth weren't seen,
nor its showering, its tenting. Just the detail
that swam in its flow-lines, glossing about—
as she paced on, comet-like, face to the sun.

Cotton Flannelette

Shake the bed, the blackened child whimpers,
O shake the bed! through beak lips that never
will come unwry. And wearily the iron-
framed mattress, with nodding crockery bulbs,
jinks on its way.
                              Her brothers and sister take
shifts with the terrible glued-together baby
when their unsleeping absolute mother
reels out to snatch an hour, back to stop
the rocking and wring pale blue soap-water
over nude bladders and blood–webbed chars.

Even their cranky evasive father
is awed to stand watches rocking the bed.
Lids frogged shut, *O please shake the bed,*
her contour whorls and braille tattoos
from where, in her nightdress, she flared
out of hearth-drowse to a marrow shriek
pedalling full tilt firesleeves in mid-air,
                              are grainier with repair
than when the doctor, crying *Dear God, woman!*
No one can save that child. Let her go!
spared her the treatments of the day.

Shake the bed. Like: count phone poles, rhyme,
classify realities, bang the head, any
iteration that will bring, in the brain's forks,
the melting molecules of relief,
and bring them again.
                              O rock the bed!

Nibble water with bared teeth, make lymph
like arrowroot gruel, as your mother grips you
for weeks in the untrained perfect language,
till the doctor relents. Salves and wraps you
in dressings that will be the fire again,
ripping anguish off agony,
                              and will confirm

the ploughland ridges in your woman's skin
for the sixty more years your family weaves you
on devotion's loom, rick-racking the bed
as you yourself, six years old, instruct them.

The Trances

We came from the Ice Age,
we work for the trances.
The hunter, the Mother,
seers' inside-out glances

come from the Ice Age,
all things in two sexes,
the priest man, the beast man,
I flatten to run
I rise to be human.

We came from the Ice Age
with the walk of the Mothers
with the walk of the powers
we walked where sea now is

we made the dry land
we told it in our trances
we burnt it with our sexes
but the tongue it is sand
see it, all dry taste buds
lapping each foot that crosses
every word is more sand.

Dup dup hey duhn duhn
the rhythm of the Mothers.
We come from the Ice Ages
with the tribes and the trances
the drum's a tapped drone
dup dup hey duhn duhn.

We come from the Ice Age,
poem makers, homemakers,
how you know we are sacred:
it's unlucky to pay us.

Kings are later, farmers later.
After the Ice Age, they
made landscape, made neuter,
they made prose and pay.

Things are bodied by the trances,
we must be paid slant,
loved, analysed and scorned,
the priest's loved in scorn,
how you know he is sacred.

We're gifted and pensioned.
Some paid ones were us:
when they got their wages
ice formed in their mouths
chink chink, the Ice Age.

A prose world is the Ice Age
it is all the one sex
and theory, that floats land
we came over that floe land

we came from the Ice Age
we left it by the trances
worlds warm from the trances
duhn duhn hey dup dup
it goes on, we don't stop
we walk on from the Ice Age.

The Warm Rain

Against the darker trees or an open car shed
is where we first see rain, on a cumulous day,
a subtle slant locating the light in air
in front of a forties still of tubs and bike-frames.

Next sign, the dust that was white pepper bared
starts pitting and re-knotting into peppercorns.
It stops being a raceway of rocket smoke behind cars,
it sidles off foliage, darkens to a lustre. The roof
of the bush barely leaks yet, but paper slows right down.

Hurrying parcels pearl but don't now split
crossing the carparks. People clap things in odd salute
to the side of their heads, yell wit, dance on their doubles.
The sunny parallels, when opposite the light, have a flung look
like falling seed. They mass, and develop a shore sound:
fixtures get cancelled, the muckiest shovels rack up.

The highway whizzes, and lorries put spin on vapour:
soon puddles hit at speed will arch over you like a slammed sea.
I love it all, I agree with it. At nightfall, the cause
of the whole thing revolves, in white and tints, on TV
like the Crab nebula: it brandishes palm trees like mops,
its borders swell over the continent, they compress the other
nations of the weather. Fruit bumps lawn, and every country dam

brews under bubbles, milky temperas sombering to oils.
Grass rains upward; the crepe-myrtle tree heels, sopping crimson,
needing to be shaken like the kilt of a large man.
Hills run, air and paddocks are swollen. Eaves dribble like jaws
and coolness is a silent film, starring green and mirrors.

Tiny firetail finches, quiet in our climber rose, agree to it
like early humans. Cattle agree harder, hunched out in the clouds.
From here, the ocean may pump up and up and explode
around the lighthouses in gigantic cloak sleeves, the whole book
of foam slide and fritter, disclosing a pen shaft. Paratroops

of salt water may land in dock streets, skinless balloons
be flat out to queue down every drain, and the wind race
thousands of flags. Or we may be just chirpings, damped
under calm high cornfields of pour, with butter clearings

that spread and resume glare, hiding the warm rain
back inside our clothes, as mauve trees scab to cream
and grey trees strip bright salmon, with loden patches.

Demo

No. Not from me. Never.
Not a step in your march,
not a vowel in your unison,
bray that shifts to bay.

Banners sailing a street river,
power in advance of a vote,
go choke on these quatrain tablets.
I grant you no claim ever,

not if you pushed the Christ Child
as president of Rock Candy Mountain
or yowled for the found Elixir
would your caste expectations snare me.

Superhuman with accusation,
you would conscript me to a world
of people spat on, people hiding
ahead of oncoming poetry.

Whatever class is your screen
I'm from several lower.
To your rigged fashions, I'm pariah.
Nothing a mob does is clean,

not at first, not when slowed to a media,
not when police. The first demos I saw,
before placards, were against me,
alone, for two years, with chants,

every day, with half-conciliatory
needling in between, and aloof
moral cowardice holding skirts away.
I learned your world order then.

The Genetic Galaxy

for Sir John Guise

In many a powerless mind
lurks this chart, wider than the world,
maybe vast enough to wrap Earth in,
which diagrams with merciless truth
the parentage of everyone, identified
and linked with their real blood kin
across all of time and space.

Strips and fragments of this
have always been waved, in ribaldry
or secret, at Identity overdone,
that is, underdone with intent—
wives have hung them out with the smalls,
Hitler sent Panzers to train
all over his, for Gentility.

Certain knowledge or the insurrection
of guesswork, month-counter's revenge, the
mugging of high sentence by and with
its impossible relations—plenty
if they could get the true chart
wouldn't care that to display it entire
might be ridiculous and terrible:

Howls of revised posh, unspoken people,
cousinship with kulak-shooters, death-rays
of Whititude and Negritude, burning wills,
anguish of men out of whose children
other men peer innocently,
shock historical non-paternities
and the stratosphere-tightening
gasp at incest seen in full.

Glorious to see a hero car-bomber
shattered by wrong ancestry, a Klan klutz

awed by strata of peoples, all his,
or an adoptee hunched, devouring names,
but the chart would need to hang
in Space, to be safe from us,
like the relativised stars, which were
once also made by love.

A million years' unreachable blamed dead
might stun revenge, sheer wealth of tangents
heal affinity and victimhood:
an Indigenous poet might regain her
Hispano-Scots Kanak dimensions, as her
scorners darkly complexified.
She's your aunt a thousand generations
before your sealblubber aunts, Son of Heaven.

A species-deep net of anecdote
with every life its pardon.
In that weak Force I'm one eighth
of a musketeer, being slightly a Dumas
on my Aboriginal side. The chart is always
odder than reincarnation's princess tales
with truncations and tears. It's the galaxy
we are making, the kinship sum:
I'm game to see it. I want it to come.

Blowfly Grass

The houses those suburbs could afford
were roofed with old savings books, and some
seeped gravy at stitches in their walls;

some were clipped as close as fury,
some grimed and corner-bashed by love
and the real estate, as it got more vacant,

grew blady grass and blowfly grass, so called
for the exquisite lanterns of its seed,
and the land sagged subtly to a low point,

it all inclined way out there to a pit
with burnt-looking cheap marble edges
and things and figures flew up from it

like the stones in the crusher Piers had
for making dusts of them for glazes:
flint, pyroclase, slickensides, quartz, schist,

snapping, refusing, and spitting high
till the steel teeth got gritty corners on them
and could grip them craw-chokingly to grind.

It's their chance, a man with beerglass-cut arms
told me. Those hoppers got to keep filled. A girl,
edging in, bounced out cropped and wrong-coloured

like a chemist's photo, crying. Who could blame her
among in-depth grabs and Bali flights and phones?
She was true, and got what truth gets.

The Head-Spider

Where I lived once, a roller coaster's range
of timber hills peaked just by our backyard cliff
and cars undulated scream-driven round its seismograph
and climbed up to us with an indrawn gasp of girls.

Smiles and yelling could be exchanged as they crested
then they'd pitch over, straining back in a shriek
that volleyed as the cars were snatched from sight
in the abyss, and were soon back. Weekdays they rested,

and I rested all days. There was a spider in my head
I'd long stay unaware of. If you're raped you mostly know
but I'd been cursed, and refused to notice or believe it.
Aloof in a Push squat, I thought I was moral, or dead.

Misrule was strict there, and the Pill of the day only ever
went into one mouth, not mine, and foamed a Santa-beard.
I was resented for chastity, and slept on an overcoat.
Once Carol from upstairs came to me in bra and kindness

and the spider secreted by girls' derision-rites to spare
women from me had to numb me to a crazed politeness.
Squeals rode the edge of the thrill building. Cartoonist Mercier
drew springs under Sydney. Push lovers were untrue on principle.

It's all architecture over there now. A new roller coaster
flies its ups and downs in wealth's face like an affront.
I've written a new body that only needs a reader's touch.
If love is cursed in us, then when God exists, we don't.

The Push: An Australian bohemia existing from the 1940s to the 1970s. Nominally
libertarian, it in fact enforced a fairly pedantic inversion of ordinary norms and prac-
tices. Its most famous alumna is Germaine Greer.

▌ Dreambabwe

Streaming, a hippo surfaces
like the head of someone
lifting, with still-entranced eyes,
from a lake of stanzas.

One Kneeling, One Looking Down

Half-buried timbers chained corduroy
lead out into the sand
which bare feet wincing Crutch and Crotch
spurn for the summer surf's embroidery
and insects stay up on the land.

A storm engrossing half the sky
in broccoli and seething drab
and standing on one foot over the country
burrs like lit torch. Lightning
turns air to elixir at every grab

but the ocean sky is untroubled blue
everywhere. Its storm rolls below:
sand clouds raining on sacred country
drowned a hundred lifetimes under sea.
In the ruins of a hill, channels flow,

and people, like a scant palisade
driven in the surf, jump or sway
or drag its white netting to the tide line
where a big man lies with his limbs splayed,
fingers and toes and a forehead-shine

as if he'd fallen off the flag.
Only two women seem aware of him.
One says *But this frees us. I'd be a fool—*
Say it with me, says the other. *For him to revive*
we must both say it. Say: Be alive.—

   But it was our own friends who got
   him with a brave shot, a clever shot.—
   Those are our equals: we scorn them
   for being no more than ourselves.
   Say it with me. Say: Be alive.—

   Elder sister, it is impossible.—
   Life was once impossible. And flight. And speech.

It was impossible to visit the moon.
The impossible's our summoning dimension.
Say it with me. Say: Be alive again.—

The younger wavers. She won't leave
nor stop being furious. The sea's vast
catchment of light sends ashore a roughcast
that melts off every swimmer who can stand.
Glaring through slits, the storm moves inland.

The younger sister, wavering, shouts *Stay dead!*
She knows how impossibility
is the only door that opens.
She pities his fall, leg under one knee
but her power is his death, and can't be dignified.

Bottles in the Bombed City

They gave the city a stroke. Its memories
are cordoned off. They could collapse on you.

Water leaks into bricks of the Workers' century
and every meaning is blurred. No word in Roget

now squares with another. If the word is Manchester
it may be Australia, where that means sheets and towels.

To give the city a stroke, they mixed a lorryload
of henbane and meadowsweet oil and countrified her.

Now Engels supports Max, and the British Union
of beautiful ceramics is being shovelled up,

blue-green tiles of the Corn Exchange,
umber gloss bricks of the Royal Midlands Hotel.

Unmelting ice everywhere, and loosened molecules.
When the stroke came, every bottle winked at its neighbour.

The Margin of Difference

One and one make two,
the literalist said.
So far they've made five billion,
said the lateralist, or ten
times that, if you count the dead.

The Harleys

Blats booted to blatant
dubbin the avenue dire
with rubbings of Sveinn Forkbeard
leading a black squall of Harleys
with Moe Snow-Whitebeard and

Possum Brushbeard and their ladies
and, sphincter-lipped, gunning,
massed leather muscle on a run,
on a roll, Santas from Hell
like a whole shoal leaning

wide-wristed, their tautness stable
in fluency, fast streetscape dwindling,
all riding astride, on the outside
of sleek grunt vehicles, woman-clung,
forty years on from Marlon.

Aurora Prone

The lemon sunlight poured out far between things
inhabits a coolness. Mosquitoes have subsided,
flies are for later heat.
Every tree's an auburn giant with a dazzled face
and the back of its head to an infinite dusk road.
Twilights broaden away from our feet too
as rabbits bounce home up defiles in the grass.
Everything widens with distance, in this perspective.
The dog's paws, trotting, rotate his end of infinity
and dam water feels a shiver few willow drapes share.
Bright leaks through their wigwam re-purple the skinny beans
then rapidly the light tops treetops and is shortened
into a day. Everywhere stands pat beside its shadow
for the great bald radiance never seen in dreams.

The Instrument

Who reads poetry? Not our intellectuals;
they want to control it. Not lovers, not the combative,
not examinees. They too skim it for bouquets
and magic trump cards. Not poor schoolkids
furtively farting as they get immunized against it.

Poetry is read by the lovers of poetry
and heard by some more they coax to the café
or the district library for a bifocal reading.
Lovers of poetry may total a million people
on the whole planet. Fewer than the players of skat.

What gives them delight is a never-murderous skim
distilled, to verse mainly, and suspended in rapt
calm on the surface of paper. The rest of poetry
to which this was once integral still rules
the continents, as it always did. But on condition now

that its true name is never spoken. This, feral poetry,
the opposite but also the secret of the rational,
who reads that? Ah, the lovers, the schoolkids,
debaters, generals, crime-lords, everybody reads it:
Porsche, lift-off, Gaia, Cool, patriarchy.

Among the feral stanzas are many that demand your flesh
to embody themselves. Only completed art
free of obedience to its time can safely conduct you
through and athwart the larger poems you are in.
Being outside all poetry is an unreachable void.

Why write poetry? For the weird unemployment.
For the painless headaches, that must be tapped to strike
down along your writing arm at the accumulated moment.
For the adjustments after, aligning facets in a verb
before the trance leaves you. For working always beyond

your own intelligence. For not needing to rise
and betray the poor to do it. For a non-devouring fame.

Little in politics resembles it: perhaps
the Australian colonists' re-inventing of the snide
far-adopted secret ballot, in which deflation could hide

and, as a welfare bringer, shame the mass-grave Revolutions,
so axe-edged, so lictor-y.
Was that moral cowardice's one shining world victory?
Breathing in dream-rhythm awake and far from bed
evinces the gift. Being tragic with a book on your head.

Rodd Island Wedding

On your wedding day, women were seated
on the Harbour, resting their oars.
Single sculls, in the grace of that spelling,
their canoes, slim as compass needles
pointed at sandstone black with water,
at balconies and wharves and houses,
at sunny bays and lawn-set madhouses,
those châteaux of the upper Harbour,
at the tensioned bridges and their opposites.

Aqaba! A snorkel cleared its throat
and there you were, facing castanets of focus
on your wedding island. Since you'd become happy,
you told me, you'd stopped writing poems.
I should wish you a long silence. I do,
I do, if you mean it. The ribbed iron
feast-hall cruised through courses and clapping
like an airship under fans. The sportswomen
bent, and knitted water in spaced cable-stitch.

Coolongolook Timber Mill

Down a road padlocked now
steel discs and weeds sprawled
in a room whose rusty hair
was iron cornrows, and its brow

a naily timber lintel
under which I'd gaze across
the river at Midge Island
as the tide turned on its pintle

and atoms would be dancing
like mayflies in the dusk
at the exact same speed as
gold roubles once spread glancing

around inch-freeboard puntloads
of sleepers axe trimmed
for Wittgenstein and Company
building the Siberian railroads

and black saws' sharkmouth edges
kept pipe-stuffers careful
up skids from sawdust-sized
shimmering of midges

then living drills were screwed
from punk wood to eat
by men wearing genitals; their
fish spears twitched like sedges

and the ocean sprawled in sight
gull-squealing, then weeks away
and the night sky quivered
with the vanished river's fleet

—a city man bought
the mill land for ten times
its price, and let the mill
fall down. But I have kept it.

▌Incunabular

Tom Fisher was my Grail King:
he endowed the Gothic library
to which my life had been pointing.
His high sandstone box held the Culture
bush folk were scorned for lacking.

On its milk-glass stack levels I still
hear stiletto heels clacking,
glass floors for the light to perfuse,
not for voyeurs: you could only
make out the sex of shoes.

The lipsticked gargoyle downstairs
kissed much social ascent.
Above, I'd browse beside the point
power made, for the points it didn't.
Reflex, more than intent.

The reading-room beams supported heraldry
and a roof like a steep tent.
Mine was a plan-free mass querying
of condensed humans off the shelves,
all numbered, the tribal, the elderly.

Knowledge was the gait of compressed selves
and poetry seemed windows of italic
inset in grievous prose
which served it and mastered it:
few grapes for many rows.

Students murmured airily of the phallic
they were going to be marked by
but the shelvers book-trolleys were parked by
closed gaping tomes and stood them drily back,
vogue, value, theory.

The stacks clanged down metal stairs
to floors below reality,

to books in dragon-buckram, books like dreams,
antiphonaries and grimoires,
philologies with pages still uncut:

my blade made a sound like *rut*.
I never used the catalogue,
it held no serendipities.
The lateral book's the tip: it is
the seminal one near the one set.

You must range real shelves to find it.
Strict exams could have excluded me;
soon they did weed out my sort.
Critique closed over poetry,
the hip proved very straight.

What our donjon of kisses and cribs held
they say now will go on line.
This does not light my taper.
Others may have my joys at home? Fine.
But I surfed the true paper.

To Me You'll Always Be Spat

Baby oyster, little grip,
settling into your pinch of shape
on a flooded timber rack:

little living gravel
I'm the human you need,
one who won't eat you,

not with much relish, even
when you're maturely underexercised
inside your knuckle sandwich.

Bloodless sheep's eye, never
appear in a bottle. Always bring
ice, lemon and your wonky tub.

You have other, non-food powers:
your estuaries are kept clean as crystal,
you eat through your jacuzzi,

you make the non-sexy
think of a reliable wet
machine of pleasure,

truly inattentive students
of French hope they heard right,
that you chant in the arbours.

Commandant-of-convicts Wallis
who got the Wallis name unfairly
hated, had you burnt alive

in millions to make mortar.
May you now dance in the streets
and support a gross of towns!

The Disorderly

We asked How old will you be
in the year Two Thousand?
Sixty-two. Sixty. Fifty-nine.

Unimaginable. We started running
to shin over the sliprails
of a wire fence. You're last!—

It's alright: I'll be first in Heaven!
and we jogged on to school
past a yellow-flowering guinea vine.

Cattle stood propped on the mountain.
We caught a day-blind glider possum
and took him to school. Only later

at the shoe-wearing edge of our world
did we meet kids who thought everything
ridiculous. They found us incredible.

Cream-handed men in their towns
never screamed Christ-to-Jesus! at the hills
with diabetes breath, nor talked fight

or Scotch poetry in scared timber rooms.
Such fighters had lost, we realised
but we had them to love

or else we'd be mongrels.
This saved our souls later on,
sometimes, crossing the cousinless

detective levels of the world
to the fat-free denim culture,
that country of the Attitudes.

Five Postcards

Having run herself up out of
plush, the white-cheeked wallaby
sits between her haunches
like an old-country tailor behind
her outstretched last yard, her tail,
and hems it with black fingers.

Cosmic apples by Cézanne:
their colours, streaming, hit
wavelengths of crimson and green
in the yellow particle-wind.
Slant, parallel and pouring,
every object's a choke-point of speeds.

The kitchens of this eighteenth-century
Oxford college are ten metres high
by the squinch-eyed cooks basting
tan birds spiked in hundreds all over
the iron griddle before hellfire.
Below high lozengy church windows
others flour, fill, pluck. And this too
was the present once, that absolute of fools.

1828. Timber slums of the future
top a ship of the line, which receives
more who might have stormed St James's.
Cheery washing lines signal they're bound
for the world's end, to seize there
the lands of unclothed aristos
rich in myth and formal grammar.

A mirrory tar-top road across
a wide plain. Drizzling sky.
A bike is parked at a large book

turned down tent-fashion on the verge.
One emerging says *I read such crazy
things in this book. 'Every bird
has stone false teeth, and enters
the world in its coffin.' That's in there.*

Index of Titles

Index of First Lines